Tour of Flanders:
The Inside Story

The rocky roads of the
Ronde van Vlaanderen

Les Woodland

McGann Publishing
Cherokee Village, Arkansas

Published by McGann Publishing
P.O. Box 576
Cherokee Village, AR 72525
USA
www.mcgannpublishing.com

McGann
Publishing

ISBN 978-0-9859636-2-0
Printed in the United States of America

Cover photo: The race ascends the Molenberg in 2009.

Bike-racing is rooted in the Belgian, and particularly Flemish, character at a depth that no Italian sports can begin to approach. Watching a great race in Flanders, one can feel oneself entering the soul of a people; a rather dour soul at that, it must be added.

—Robin Magowan

The results of all Tours of Flanders can be found on the publisher's website, www.BikeRaceInfo.com

Map of Belgium

showing the
principal cities
visited by the
Tour of Flanders

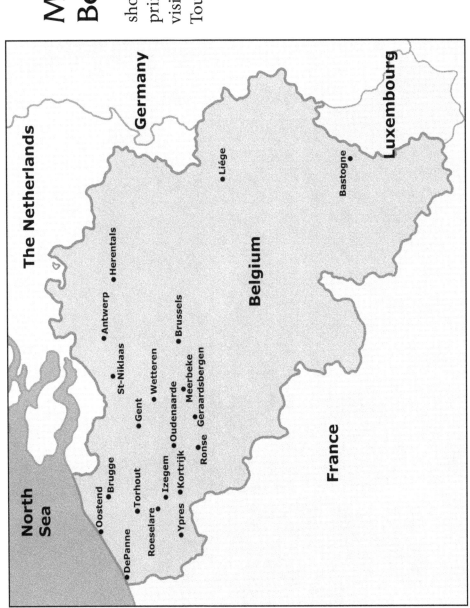

Well, be brave, Belgian boys; be brave and irresistible in the fight against the foreign champions. Defend our honor and reputation and when you return to the motherland, we will acclaim you as you deserve and you'll hear thousands of chests swell and shout: "Hooray, the Belgian champion!"

—Karel van Wijnendaele, founder of the Ronde van Vlaanderen

1
All Those Yellow
Flags With Lions

Being a policeman on the Tour de France isn't easy. It's a job that anyone could fancy. Anyone without the talent to actually ride the race, that is. But you're out in all weather on your motorbike, colder or hotter than the riders because you're not moving. You're riding at a fraction of what the giant machine beneath you can manage, holding it like a bridled stallion. You can't stop for a pee like the riders do. You don't get to see much racing. And there are unrivaled opportunities to take everyone the wrong way.

(Or indeed to be falsely accused of it: Robert Millar took the wrong route in the Tour de France of 1988 and lost a stage in the mountains, then blamed a gendarme for sending him the wrong way. As it happened, he picked on a rather jolly chap who'd done the job for years, a favorite of riders and spectators alike, and who took the accusation so personally that he went to ask Millar why he had done it. The world sided with the policeman; Millar belatedly accepted that it was his own mistake.)

A decade or two back I stood beside the road when a Tour stage finished in Brighton, a raucous holiday town on the English south coast. To be precise, it was on July 6, 1994. The riders had been going for four days and their last stint on the continent had been a team time-trial from Calais to the tunnel that takes trains beneath the Channel to England. That may not seem all that far, given that the tunnel starts only just outside Calais, but the riders had gone a longer way round. They had hot wax in their shorts and 67 kilometers in their legs by the time they were allowed to find the chartered train that would take them to Dover, just about in sight across 40 kilometers of gray water.

To reach us in Brighton had taken another 205 kilometers because once again the riders had taken the schoolboy route. News had reached us that the favorite, a tall but dull Spaniard called Miguel Indurain, had told reporters that the climbs he most feared in this Tour were in the Alps, the Pyrenees, "and the climb of Ditchling Beacon." He said it either with dry humor or as a diplomat. Because Ditchling Beacon isn't even the highest hill in the South Downs hills, just behind Brighton. It's the third highest, a pimply 248 meters with just 158 meters of actual climbing. Local amateurs puff their way up on Sunday afternoons and many of the several thousand participants in the London–Brighton bike ride get off and walk up, glad that their 87 kilometers will be over soon after they spot the sea on the other side.

That day in 1994, we read the local evening newspaper and marveled at how it had been able to describe the day's start in Kent and yet be on the streets of Brighton so quickly afterward; we laughed at Indurain's politeness and wondered if he'd even bother to get out of the saddle on Ditchling Beacon; and we milled about, thousands of us, good-humored, enjoying the sunshine but at a loose end. There were hours to go.

There wasn't much to divert us. The leggy publicity girls who usually walk up and down the finishing straight to hurl key rings and cheap cloth hats into the crowd had for the most part stayed in France. The commercial companies they were promoting hadn't seen it worth crossing the Channel to greet a people who couldn't buy their goods anyway. Without them, and still without the riders, our interest fastened on the gendarmes who'd traveled across the Channel with the riders they guarded. They looked so different from our local lads. They rode snazzier motorbikes and they wore neat, pale blue shirts with short sleeves, an outfit which had British policemen sniffing in contempt. What they didn't wear was pistols. British people aren't allowed guns and they certainly weren't going to allow them to foreigners. The gendarmes' holsters were empty.

Nor did the British police show their French visitors much grace. If a gendarme stopped in the wrong place, up would come a policeman to order him on his way. In English, or the sort of English that policemen speak. The crowd cheered. The Tour may be thoroughly French but that didn't mean there was no fun in the comeuppance of an arrogant, garlic-smelling Frenchman who had a wonderful view of the Tour, a gorgeous pouting mistress and a lot of Sacha Distel records. Because that, everyone knew, was what Frenchmen were like. Even policemen.

In Belgium, they were mildly upset by all this *lèse-majesté*. Belgians honored the Tour. Tradition holds that it should cross into its northern neighbor most years if only for a day. In 1994 it hadn't been possible to go there and to ride in England as well. Belgians know about cycle racing and what they know includes that the British know nothing at all. So why go to a damp island out in the North Sea, a place which had never supplied a winner but had twice provided the man in last place, when Belgians had always done so well? For three days, men sat in bars all over Belgium, sulked and refused to take an interest until the Tour returned to the mainland.

When the Tour goes to Belgium, the Belgians let French gendarmes travel with guns and they treat them as their own. I stood by the road at a stage of the Tour in Belgium once and watched a bunch of happy fans hand the gendarmes some of those yellow flags you see all over the place there, the ones with the rampant black lion. The French policemen were happy to play along and show good will and there was a cheer when they clipped the flags to their motorbikes and rode away.

Back at the police office there were solemn words waiting. As my friend Willy said—all Belgian men of a certain age are called Willy— "They just saw a pretty flag, the one at bike races they'd watched on television. They were delighted the crowd cheered. People don't often cheer policemen. What they didn't know was that the crowd were cheering not them but because the yellow flag is the symbol of Flanders and Flemish independence." The French government, through the unwitting and admittedly minor path of its gendarmerie, had just lent its support to the disintegration of Belgium.

Because that's Belgium: a kingdom the size of Maryland or East Anglia, divided by language and custom and doomed, say pessimists, to tear itself apart. It will be shredded by seemingly irreparable differences between the Dutch-speaking north and the French-speaking south. Because while the world finds Belgium's short history of no interest, Belgians are obsessed by it. Their differences define their whole.

And you have to understand that to understand the Tour of Flanders, the Ronde van Vlaanderen. Because otherwise little of the story makes sense. You see, those yellow flags with black lions aren't just the color of the Ronde: they stand for a century of suppression and escape, for poverty and prosperity, and even for claims of collaboration with the Nazis. And out of all that, the Ronde was born.

So, where to start? Well, probably with the unforgettably named Leopold Georg Christian Friederich von Sachen-Coburg-Saalfeld, Duke of Saxony. He looked just as splendid as his name, too, with a

Leopold—a Russian colonel when he was five, heir to the British throne and finally King of the Belgians.

high forehead, a strong but not dominant nose, thin lips that could smile and sneer equally easily, and an unusual habit of brushing his thick black hair forward rather than back and letting it run down the side of his face in sideburns that would have done the 1970s proud.

Léo, as I'll call him to save ink and eyesight, was born in Germany nine days before Christmas in 1790. He became a colonel in the Russian guards when he was only five. He must have been good because by 12 he was made a major-general. So good that Napoleon asked him to help run the French army, although admittedly not at 12 years old. He said no, went back to Russia and fought the French.

Then he sided with the British. In 1816 he married a beak-nosed lass named Charlotte Augusta, the only legitimate daughter of George IV. That made him second in line for the British throne. Charlotte was a challenge for her husband, having been described in her childhood as a feisty, headstrong tomboy. But his hopes to be king died just as quickly as his wife, who perished at 21 after producing a stillborn son shortly before their second wedding anniversary.

That left Léo free to look around again. Greece asked him to be king, but he declined. And then in 1831, having already married for a second time and being on the point of marrying yet again, he got a call from Belgium. It too was casting about for a monarch on becoming an independent country and it suggested that he give it a go. And so on 21 July 1831, Léo became the first King of the Belgians, a reign that lasted 34 years. He wasn't, you'll notice, king of Belgium but King of the Belgians. That's how it is in Belgium.

But there his luck ran out. Two weeks later the Dutch swept into his new country to sort out a revolution and it took eight years to get them out again.

It's worth going into that because otherwise it's hard to understand the Ronde. You see, Léo got rid of the Dutch with the help of the French. France had been upset about the Netherlands ever since losing the country in a battle in 1813. Disgruntlement meant Napoleon was happy to help clear the Dutch out of Belgium and that influence still further confirmed French as a language, a culture and a debt. To this day, the king of the Belgians speaks French as his first language.

"First" language because Belgium has three. There is an enclave of German-speakers near Liège but they, for our story, can be forgotten.

The main languages are French and Dutch. Flemish, as it's often called, is Dutch by a different name and accent. Belgians use a few different words and have a habit of going up at the end of sentences but Dutchmen and Belgians understand each other perfectly. "Flemish" refers more to a culture than a language and so, from now on, I'll call the language Dutch. Although I'll have to refer to the people as Flemish or Flemings or as Flandrians.

The language divide between French and Dutch runs horizontally across the country. Find Brussels, the capital, and draw a roughly horizontal line through it across the country. Everyone above it will speak Dutch and those below it will speak French.

French is a world language but Dutch is spoken only in the Netherlands, its former colonies and in northern Belgium. Aristocrats in Brussels therefore had no interest in learning it. To them it was a petty, guttural and useless language not worth their consideration.

More, it embarrassed a nation determined to build a future. It confused northern Belgium with the Netherlands, it sounded ugly and nobody wanted to speak it. French was the world's language of enlightenment and literature and, until the Treaty of Versailles that those early Belgians couldn't have predicted, when English got its first grip, the single language of global democracy. How much more sensible to make Flemings speak French than let them ramble in whatever nonsense it was that they spoke up there. And so Brussels tried to squash the language and banned its teaching and even printing. Belgian Dutch collapsed into dialects, sometimes incomprehensible between regions. French was imposed on the north but few there mastered it except in a handful of areas, such as Gent, where it had a snob value.

Gilles Comte, the editor of the French magazine, *Vélo*, wrote: "At the start of the [20th] century, West Flanders was a dead country. Condemned to misery, young people took to their bikes to go to harvest beetroot on the other side of the border."

Briek Schotte, a man who would become a saint to these men, said: "A Flandrian, that was a rider who respected nobody, who fought on and on. A lot of West Flandrians used to go off for a week with a sort of rucksack on their back, to work where they could, in brick ovens, bringing in the harvest. They were mercenaries, nomads, abandoned by God and man alike. They slept on the road, in the gutter, or in the hay at some farmer's. They were loners, workers who thought selling their labor by the day was nothing exceptional."

They were so rough and hard-edged that the 1913 six-day on the track in Brussels, the second there with two-man teams, ended in a brawl. The exclusively French-speaking national cycling federation was sure it knew where the problem lay. It wrote in its report that "the Flemish must acquire, whatever the cost, a bit of civility, without which we will never be able to work with these semi-savages."

Things became bitterest in the world war of 1914–18, although ironically the German occupiers saw the Flemish as oppressed and restored their right to use Dutch in schools. In the Belgian army, though, things were different. Northern soldiers found themselves under officers who spoke only French. It never seemed to happen the other way round. Misunderstandings and resentment were mutual. And heated.

As one chronicler observed: "Ordinary Flemish soldiers were now dying to save Flanders and with it Belgium, while all the time being given orders in French by their officers. The sentiment began to grow that if Flemish blood was good enough to be spilt for Belgium then their language was good enough to be spoken there. King Albert was openly addressed by his soldiers, but at a time when Russia was in political turmoil and militant activists seemed to be everywhere (helped along, needless to say, by the Germans who occupied the rest of Flanders), the king felt that the time was just not right."

To add insult, slaughtered Flemish soldiers were given headstones with a French inscription: *Mort pour la Patrie.* Dead for the Fatherland. Flemish soldiers put up their own stones with the crossed letters VVK and AVV—in translation, Flanders for Christ, All for Flanders. Then they went further. They built a crypt for one of their cultural leaders and on it, at Diksmuide, they engraved: "*Hier ons bloed; wanneer ons recht?*"—Here is our blood; when do we get out rights? It proved too much. The cross was blown up. Nobody was charged.

It suits modern Flemish separatists to insist that 80 per cent of Belgians at the front were Flemish, making them cannon fodder while French-speaking Walloons stayed behind the action in relative safety. But Sophie De Schaepdrijver, associate professor of European history at Pennsylvania State University, author of a history of the war, says that while the proportion is still hard to calculate, it was more like 65 per cent. More than 50 per cent, less than 80, but still enough to produce a good sulk. And so a sullen resentment spread across the north. And the north, just fields and the cold North Sea, grew poorer. The south, with steel, coal, business and power, grew richer. So said the Flemings. But, as ever, legend has to be generously diluted with truth.

Life, of course, went on. People worked their small farms with horses and ate what they produced and sold the rest. They rode bicycles on the flat, bleak roads and they grew passionate about cycle racing. Some of the best riders went south into France to try their hand there. Flandrians grew up, fell in love, married and increased often already large families. One reason Flanders separated from Holland was that its Catholic faith contrasted with the Calvinistic Protestantism of the Netherlands.

And the north had its own newspapers, in Dutch. One, *Sportwereld*, appeared in 1912. Its founder was a man called Karel van Wijnendaele. His memorial stands now on the route of the Tour of Flanders, the race he founded.

The author Rik Vanwalleghem, the head of the Tour of Flanders museum in Oudenaarde, says of him: "History, whether good or bad, could once be created by an individual rather than the mass. In politics, religion, art, law, sport and the economy, in other words in every form of human activity, there sometimes appear groundbreaking figures who set things on their head, question established beliefs, leave the trodden path. And some pay for their dreams with their life. Karel Steyaert, alias Karel van Wijnendaele, alias Marc Bolle, was just such a great and innovative spirit."

Some confusion here. Which *was* the man's name? Was it van Wijnendaele or Steyaert? Or Marc Bolle? The answer is that he was born Carolus Ludovicius Steyaert—pronounced *Stay-yart*—on November 16, 1882. Karel was a friendly shortening of his first name and equates in English to Charles or even Charlie. It was rounded off to "Koarle." He adopted the name van Wijnendaele for his writing and it's how he's best known to this day. Marc Bolle was a name he adopted first as a rider and then as a riders' agent. From now on, unless there's a good reason not to, I'll refer to him as Karel van Wijnendaele.

Karel was the fifth of 15 children. He was born in Bakvoorde, a perfectly missable place between Torhout and Lichtervelde. The two neighboring towns were rivals. Only one could prosper from the coming of the railway—and it went, with a busy junction station, to

Karel van Wijnendaele, revered in Belgium as the father of the Ronde.

Lichtervelde. Torhout took the blow painfully; the absence of a decent rail service meant it lost its shoe factories to Izegem, 25 kilometers to the south.

He never knew his father. Petrus Steyaert (Steyaert was Karel's real name, remember) was a flax worker who died 18 months after Karel was born. He was 38. Karel never lost the bitterness of being robbed of a father, although it lessened with age. It's not obvious that his mother, Ludovica Defever, was having an affair but it took only a year for her to marry a local farmer, Richard Defreyne. She and her children moved to Smissestraat in Torhout, close to the chateau of Wijnendaele—*Way-n'n-dah-le*. Richard was keener on his new wife than on her children and their upbringing fell to her. He wasn't the sort to work hard when he didn't need to. Ludovica, on the other hand, never stopped working round the house, cooking meals, cleaning, tending to rabbits and serving beer—because the family house was also a bar.

Karel wrote in 1942: "Being born into a poor family, that was my strength. If you're brought up without frills and you know what hunger is, it makes you hard enough to withstand bike races."

He walked three kilometers to school "because trams were only things we'd heard of and bicycles were as rare as white mice." He was a bright kid. Belgium didn't demand children have more than a primitive schooling. Most left at 12 to work on the land or in factories, shops or offices in Torhout. That was how his mother wanted it, telling Karel at 12 that school was finished and that now he'd be the man of the house and work and look after the rest of the children. Karel loved the idea— "no more awkward questions to answer" at school—and that's how it would have been had a clergyman not persuaded his mother that he showed promise and that he should stay at school until he was 14.

Clergymen had strong roots in Torhout because, as early as the ninth century, the town had sent missionaries across pagan Europe. One of them, a monk known as Rimbert, or Rembert, became archbishop of Hamburg-Bremen in 865. It was a job he inherited from his friend and travel companion, Ansgar. Rimbert died in Bremen in 888 and was made a saint. Torhout is proud of its history.

It wasn't the church to which Karel turned when he left school, however. He had the strong Catholic beliefs that were then part of rural Flemish life, a world of dutiful devotion and large families, but he went to work instead in his stepfather's fields. Then, frustrated by that, he moved through various jobs such as a pharmacist's messenger boy and a program seller. He worked for a baker, washed bottles and delivered parcels. He worked for French-speaking families out on the coast and felt humiliated by how they treated him, this country boy who struggled to understand their language. And then, just after the turn of the century, he became an advocate's clerk.

The first bike track he saw was at Oostend in 1897, watching Robert Protin beat Jules Fischer and Paul Ruinart. Protin, a long-faced man with a weak chin who came from Liège close to the German border, was amateur sprint champion of Belgium for four successive years, from 1891 to 1894. He then turned professional in 1895 and

Karel would have been especially pleased that day in Oostend because Protin was not only the best in Belgium but the best in the world. He had just won the first world sprint championship. Although it didn't happen without incident.

The championship was held in Germany, in Cologne. Protin was pitched against George Banker, the son of an American tycoon and member of the Pittsburg Athletic Club, and against another Belgian, Émile Huet. It was an elite trio and the starter was more nervous than any of the riders. Legend says that, bringing down the starting flag, he poked it in Protin's eye. That reduced the competition and Banker finished the race ahead of Huet. The judges were happy to accord him the championship but the crowd sided with Protin, who was rubbing the pain out of his eyes. Belgian officials had two reasons to protest and protest they did. And they protested successfully because the judges ordered the race to be run again.

Banker saw no reason why it should be. But officials told him he wouldn't be world champion if he refused and, sullenly, he went back on the track. This time Protin won…and Banker protested that he had lost only because he was demoralized. The crowd and the International Cycling Association swung behind him and the ICA said the championship would have to be run a third time. Belgium said it would leave the ICA and maybe start a rival organization if its man didn't keep his title. (In fact it did just that, in 1900, although the revolt that created the *Union Cycliste Internationale* was more over Britain's domination.) And that was the end of it. Protin stayed world champion and Banker went home no less demoralized than he'd been before.

To return to the race that van Wijnendaele watched doubtless open-mouthed at Oostend, Jules Fischer was more a long-distance rider, winning the Belgian championship in 1893. He became a wealthy man, an aviator and winner of the 1912 Monaco hydroplane race. Paul Ruinart, "who had a fondness for strapping young lads with blond hair", as the reporter Pierre Chany put it, was a talented track rider who became an influential figure in French cycling after building his club in Paris, the Levallois, into a stable for the national road team. He was popularly known as Father La Ruine.

Van Wijnendaele watched the racing and felt inspired. He then got out his own bike and spent three years trying but failing to make it as a racing cyclist. Finishing time after time behind the leaders was upsetting for a boy who already had clear dreams of success in life. But, painful though it was, he was rational. "I wasn't a great oak like Cyrille van Hauwaert [his idol]," he wrote. "I was more a sapling of soft wood. Not succeeding on a bike was the greatest disappointment of my life, because I had bike-racing in the blood."

Van Wijnendaele was more an artist than an athlete. Two extra years at school and a chance at amateur acting had given him a love of literature. He read all he could—in Dutch, a language he reveled in speaking with a strong Flemish accent and much dialect and patois— and he began earning extra francs as local correspondent of regional newspapers and magazines. He wrote about anything but above all he recorded parish-pump news such as wedding anniversaries, church meetings and first-born children. He began reporting bike races for *De Thouroutenar*, his local paper in Torhout, and then for *Onze Kampioenen* (Our Champions) in Antwerp, *Sportvriend* (Friend of Sport) in Izegem and a general sports paper, *Het Sportblad*. And along the way he adopted the pen name of Karel van Wijnendaele.

There is a parallel here with the founder of another Tour, the Tour de France. Henri Desgrange had also been a lawyer's clerk before becoming a racer. Then, like van Wijnendaele, he became a journalist and then a race promoter, having founded a newspaper along the way. Van Wijnendaele and Desgrange each also managed a track and organized national teams. The similarity is striking. Jacques Augendre, the Tour de France's official historian, wrote in *Abécédaire Insolite du Tour*, that van Wijnendaele was "demanding, uncompromising; he imposed his authority." The description fit Desgrange equally well.

These were hard times not just in Flemish society but also, although reasonably with less significance, in cycling. The sport had fallen into such decline that there were only 125 licensed riders in the whole country. Vélodromes had closed and the country no longer organized national championships. There were no road titles in 1902, 1903 and 1904 and none on the track in 1901, 1902, 1903, 1905 or 1906.

We recognize Belgium now as a center of cycling, and Belgians as contenders for world titles and classic races. But clearly it wasn't so then. This was a different world. As the Dutch author, Fer Schroeders, noted: "Before 1900, it was in England and in France that cycling was the most popular sport. There was no still no real difference in standard then between professionals and amateurs. Sport in general, at the end of the '90s, profited from the effects of internationalization. Football and rugby in particular became more popular and everyday people grew more interested in tennis and car racing. There remained still a fashion for individualism and amateurism, values favored by Paris–Brussels and Paris–Tours.

"The organizers of cycling events were also just as keen on individual amateurism, but the financial interests of newspapers and bike makers soon had an impact on this policy. It didn't take long before factories began arranging for the best riders to use their bicycles. The English had a big share of the French market and a race won on one of their machines pushed up their sales substantially. Factories chased after winning amateurs. There quickly arose a move towards professionalism, riders being paid by factories to use their equipment."

But not in Belgium. There were Belgian bike factories, naturally, but they were small compared to elsewhere and without the money to make the most of this new fashion. Belgium was a small country, a divided country, poor in the north, and for most a bicycle was no more than transport to the factory, the fields or the mines. The roads were too bad to ride much further. And the sport was moribund. So that those who *were* determined to go further had to look elsewhere, notably to France.

Among the exodus to the south was Odilon Fransciscus Defraye. His parents, Camiel and Sidonie, lived in Rumbeke, now an eastern suburb of Roeselare on the way to Izegem. That was where Odile, as he was known, was born on July 14, 1888. Quite how he spelled his name is unclear. It could have been *Defraeye*, a variant before Dutch-language spelling was standardized in Belgium. And it could have been Odiel or Odile. Either way, he single-handedly resurrected Belgian cycling. And van Wijnendaele sanctified that elevation.

Odile Defraye—let's stick with the modern spelling—was a square-faced man with a mustache and a parting down the center of neatly waxed hair. He worked in a broom factory in Izegem. He won almost every race he rode, including the amateur Tour of Belgium. His employer, a man named Vanderkerckhove, gave him parcels and letters to deliver by bike, to help his training. Stories say that these deliveries could sometimes mean round trips of 200 kilometers.

"Fraye"—pronounced *Fray-ya*—turned professional in 1909, just in time to be sent for compulsory service in the army. That restricted his training and he rode the Tour that year with army permission but didn't finish. It was 1912 that he returned to civilian life, moving south to France like anyone else with ambition and joining the Alcyon team in their pale blue jerseys.

Things still didn't go well. Alcyon was a French company which, because of the customs tariffs that still operated in Europe, sold most of its bikes within France. Its sales had risen from 3,000 in 1902, when an engineer called Edmond Gentil opened his factory at Neuilly-sur-Seine, to 40,000 in 1909. The sales people liked that and they wanted a Tour team of just French riders. Defraye was to be left at home. Apart from the fact that he was Belgian, he was eccentric and unreliable. In 1913, for instance, he won Milan–San Remo and then lost all his winnings in a single night of gambling.

Defraye would have been kicking his heels at home when the rest of the team went to Paris for the Tour had Gentil not received a cross message from his distributor in western Belgium, a businessman called Bonte. "My job is hard enough as it is because of customs charges," Bonte told Gentil and his team manager, Ludo Feuillet. "Do you intend to make it still harder for me by leaving your star Belgian at home?"

Gentil saw the point—and the commercial considerations—and didn't mind reversing his decision. But he did bet both ways by insisting that Defraye ride for the team's leading Frenchman, the stick-thin Gustave Garrigou. An order, incidentally, which went against the Tour's rules that even riders in the same team weren't allowed to cooperate.

The 1912 Tour de France was the tenth. It had grown into a healthy child but Henri Desgrange was still defining the sport he had invented—bicycle stage racing. The historian and author, Bill McGann, says in *The Story of the Tour de France* that "Desgrange constantly tinkered with his race, with the ever-growing complexity of the rules a constantly changing minefield." A significant change that Defraye encountered was permission to use a freewheel. Desgrange always had an uneasy relationship with bicycles and, specifically, anything about them that might make his race easier for those who rode them. He may have allowed riders in 1912 to freewheel, for instance, but he never did allow derailleur gears. Those didn't come to the Tour until he fell ill and he was forced to hand the organization to Jacques Goddet, the son of his business partner.

One thing that didn't change was the way Desgrange judged his race, not on the time that riders took, which is the way we take for granted now, but on the order in which they crossed the line at the end of each day. He gave points to each rider as he finished the day regardless of the lead he had over the rider behind him or, indeed, the time he had lost on the rider in front. In that sense, the overall competition was judged in the way that the sprinters' competition is assessed today. Desgrange's reasoning was that if he insisted that riders stop to repair their bikes and therefore show their independence and resilience, he couldn't reasonably penalize them for the time that it took. Riders in those days were often scattered over several hours each day, so the time it took to replace a tire, for instance, was less significant than it would be now. But it still counted.

Riders, though, weren't foolish. They realized there was little point in chasing rivals they couldn't catch if they were just going to get the same points anyway. Since riders could be spread along the road by two or three hours, judging the race on points could often turn the race into a procession. Only in the last hour would riders start racing, and then only cautiously. Why exert effort in the first three-quarters of the day if it produced no advantage? And that just aggravated Desgrange even more, an anger which lives on in the daily time limit that we know today.

Defraye stuck by his instructions to help Garrigou. Until Garrigou, that is, could be helped no longer—and then Defraye won the Tour de France. The bike shop man in Belgium muttered "I told you so" and 10,000 people lined the streets of Roeselare when Defraye got home.

"It was a relief," one writer said. "It was as though Flanders had been suppressed by the south for so long that it no longer believed it could achieve anything. Not just in sport but anywhere. And then suddenly there you had this man, this young man—he was just 20, remember— undeniably a Flandrian, a man who spoke French only sparingly and often inaccurately, and he had won by the toil of his legs, his arms and back. Flandrians were land people. They knew the coldness of winter, the wind from the North Sea, the tiredness of effort. And therefore they knew what Defraye had achieved. And he had achieved it not for Belgium but for Flanders. They could have pride in themselves once more."

Defraye, the man who delivered parcels for a broom-maker, earned more in 3 years than a factory worker could hope for in 40. He built a house and a café with a bike track behind it. He raced again after the first world war but by then his best years had passed. He died in an old people's home in Bierges in 1965, when he was 77 and long forgotten.

The pride that he gave Belgium, though, never went. All those yellow flags with black lions show that. And it's an odd pride, one that celebrates now not only the emergence of the north over the south but also the toil in wind and rainswept fields that preceded it. Not many Belgians labor like that these days, of course, but the country is young and the people remember and celebrate their short and unhappy history. Grim doggedness is valued.

The writer, Robin Magowan, put it this way: "Judged by the crowds of Milan–San Remo, it is the Italians and not the Belgians who care most passionately about the sport. For most of us, riding a bike is an essentially good-weather, summer occupation. When we go out, it is asphalt we want rather than machine- and spine-rattling cobbles. But to the Flemish imagination, cobbles are to a surfaced road what poetry is to prose. One may not like the bump-bump-bump of the slowing down, but one can perhaps see the singular concentration it takes to keep to the crested line at the top of all this broken matter."

The Ronde is a test of character, hard and rugged. It is a part of Old Flanders: short, struggling people plodding beneath a wide, gray sky. The Ronde isn't a sprint and it isn't a climbers' race. It's a race for fighters, full of sharp and angular edges with predominant shades of gray. It's the atmosphere that makes it different from every other race. It is racing in a unique context, a context of irreplaceable elements: the hilly landscape, the cobbles and the weather.

—Joris Jacobs, journalist

2

A Race Is Born

The revival of regional pride when Defraye won the Tour de France is hard for us to imagine. A rainbow had appeared in a Flanders sky that for decades had been uniformly gray. Rik Vanwalleghem wrote: "In 1907 we had barely 125 licensed riders and six or seven tracks. By 1912 the numbers had jumped to more than 4,000 riders and more than 40 tracks." And there was commercial opportunity in all that for those who cashed in fastest. August De Maeght, a director of the *Société Belge de l'Imprimérie* in Brussels, saw an opening for a weekly sports magazine in Dutch. He was a man of influence, a town council member and later mayor of Halle, and finally a member of parliament. He worked on the idea with Leon van den Haute, an organizer of races, and with a man called Michel Mayens from Gent and another called Frans Wouters, from Leuven, a university city near Brussels. They called their new paper *Sportwereld*. Among the writers they recruited from all over Flanders was the man who became its most prominent cycling writer: Karel van Wijnendaele.

Van Wijnendaele said: "We thought there was a lot we could do in the area. We also wanted to publish a paper to speak to our own Flemish people in their own language and give them confidence as Flandrians. We conducted a 10-year war, for instance, with the French-speaking management of the national cycling federation in Brussels. And we won it." For a decade, Belgium's cycling administrators refused to speak Dutch to the half of the country for whom it was the native language, a fact confirmed by Briek Schotte: "Everything at the federation was in French," he said.

The paper appeared in September 1912, printing 25,000 copies. The first edition, on yellowish rather than the bright yellow paper of Desgrange's newspaper, was headed *SPORTWERELD* in thin capital italics, with smaller but more masculine capitals beneath it explaining that this was the "the organ of all sports." The four single-column pictures of the paper's founders included one of van Wijnendaele with a broad mustache and bike-fit hollows to his cheeks. He is wearing a jacket and a shirt with raised collars. The main story on the front page is about Liège–Bastogne–Liège, at that time the only race of account in Belgium. It calls it, in Dutch, Luik–Bastenaken–Luik.

Sportwereld grew quickly, appearing twice a week, then three times and soon daily. A single copy cost five centimes and an annual subscription 4 francs 50. It took over *Het Sportblad* in Antwerp and *De Sportman* and killed *De Sportvriend*. Van Wijnendaele became its editor on the first day of 1913. He was inspired by Defraye and even more by another Belgian, Cyrille van Hauwaert, from Moorslede. And he was hurt that Flanders had these good riders but no race in which to show them off. The Championship of Flanders—which began in 1908—was a good race, he reasoned, but it lacked character, it lacked significance. The French-speaking south had had Liège–Bastogne–Liège since 1892. And now that he was editor, he would give Flanders the race it wanted—the race it needed. And he was on a wave: after van Hauwaert's successes, the number of racing licenses had jumped by 1912 to more than 4,000.

"*Sportwereld* gives Flanders its own race" said the paper's headline. And beneath it, in letters almost as big: "The Ronde: a product of the Flemish people and of Flemish soil." Van Wijnendaele didn't coin the term "Flanders' Finest" but he would never have objected. "There are other races," he kept writing in his flowery style, "but there is only one Ronde van Vlaanderen."

His soul-stirring yet not always grammatical writing made him a cultural legend. Joris Jacobs, who succeeded him as editor, said: "Wherever he went during the race, you could hear the crowds calling his name: *Koarle! Koarle!* He was better known than the champions he wrote about." He had an advantage, of course. Like Desgrange and *L'Auto* in the Tour de France, he could write of faraway lands—further, that is than the neighboring village which was world's end for most of his readers—and of angel-like heroes. It didn't matter whether van Wijnendaele or Desgrange or any of their writers actually *saw* what they so colorfully reported—and frequently they didn't, because few cars could manage high mountains and a good number wallowed in the mud even on the flat—it was inspiring for the bowed field worker or the flat-capped baker's boy who dreamed of beating cobbles or flattening mountains like their heroes. There was no radio, and above all no television, to show things differently. What wasn't fact could just be made up. And it was.

The success of the Ronde wasn't immediate. There were just 37 riders and five cars on the line in Gent for the start of the first race on Sunday May 25, 1913. Van Wijnendaele set them off from the Korenmarkt with the words "Gentlemen, go!" They made their way along the wide, Gothic-lined road, past the elegant Flemish buildings and the merchants' houses and the bars, and they raced clockwise round northwest Belgium, through St-Niklaas, Aalst, Oudenaarde (where the Ronde now finishes and which is known for its brown beer), through unsuspecting Ieper (Ypres)—soon to become a field of slaughter in world war one—then Kortrijk, Veurne, Oostend, Torhout, Roeselare and Brugge.

The roads were rotten, with rarely even a perfunctory cycle path.

The story of this first Tour of Flanders, then, was that 12 riders broke clear in Kortrijk and six reached the finish track. There, Arthur Maertens and Julien van Ingelghem fell off at the entrance, leaving Paul Deman to win after 12 hours 3 minutes. He had averaged 26.9 kilometers per hour, this neat-looking man with a marked parting in slightly wavy hair, large eyes, a deep voice, stumpy chin and the hint of a mustache. He had been the first *touriste-routier* to finish the Tour de France in 1911, and he went on to win Bordeaux–Paris in 1914 and Paris–Roubaix in 1920.

I'm settling on 324 kilometers for the distance of that first race. Van Wijnendaele wrote at least once that it was 370, a figure also given by a film history of the race, but nobody agrees. And by modern standards the racing was less than frantic. The whole field stopped for food at Zottegem, around a third of the distance. All except Frons Brutin. Which brought him angry words from the others, including Abel Devogelaere, the winner of the previous season's Championship of Flanders, who snarled: "We're not here just for a laugh."

And it *wasn't* a laugh. The tradition—and therefore the rule—was each rider for himself. They carried tools in a jersey pocket or in small bags beneath the saddle or strapped to their handlebars, a spare tire around the shoulders. The bikes were made of steel, strong enough to last and to withstand rough use. Modern tires weigh 200 grams but the ones that riders used back then were 500 grams. That was partly because technology was less advanced but also because thicker treads and sidewalls survived the roads. There were no following cars equipped with wheels or entire bikes to help riders. They were left to their own devices—part of the ethos of cycling as a race between men and not team mechanics. Changing a tire meant removing the wheel, tearing the tire from the rubber cement that held it to the rim, then getting a new tire in place and inflating it before returning the wheel to the frame. Cold weather and frozen fingers could make that take four minutes. A single flat could cost a victory and riders didn't take chances with lighter and more vulnerable tires.

Nor could they change bikes. The Ronde, like the Tour de France, fixed lead seals to each rider's machine and checked they were still there at the end. "Think of it as cycling's equivalent to the ring carried by racing pigeons," riders were told. A race brought to an end by a failed bike, or simply by being left behind, led to a ride to the nearest train station and a lengthy, difficult Sunday journey back home.

There is a lot of disagreement over the prizes that first year. Some accounts say the finishers shared 1,600 francs, the winner taking 500. It's impossible now to calculate what that was worth. Not only has the currency changed—the franc hasn't existed since the introduction of the euro in 2002—but, even with straight arithmetical conversion, the figure would be meaningless because the same goods weren't available. The money, we can guess, was a lot. Some say the winner pocketed what a teacher earned in a year or a manual worker in a year and a half. Whatever it was, it was more than *Sportwereld* could afford. The paper had, in Dutch, *verder gesprongen dan zijn stok lang is*—jumped further than its stick could reach, a reference to the way countrymen leaped water-filled ditches in low-lying farmland. In English, it had bitten off more than it could chew. The costs were greater than the income.

The finish was on the wooden vélodrome at Mariakerke, now an affluent suburb of Gent, a strange track with a fish pond in its center.

Hopes that spectators paying to watch would cover the prizes died when hardly anyone turned up. What they paid for their tickets matched only half the cost of putting on the race. Thinking the track was the cause, van Wijnendaele moved the finish next year to the

Paul Deman: if only half the stories were true, he'd still be remarkable.

Deske Poorter track in Evergem. With limited success: the attendance was just 20 greater.

Spectators obviously thought better of buying tickets because they could stand beside the road for nothing and find out in bars later that day who had won. Deman—his first name is sometimes written in the colloquial Flemish style of Pol—recalled: "In all my life, I never saw so many people in one place as on the day of that first Ronde van Vlaanderen. They were standing all along the route, thousands and still more thousands of cycling fans. I used to live then in Rekkem and my racing friend, Jef [short for Jozef] Vandaele, lived in Mouscron. So we were neighbors of a sort. We were agreed that we'd ride this Ronde van Vlaanderen and we'd ride everyone off our wheel and share the prizes and prime bonuses. And then Vandaele had a flat tire. I waited for him but the bunch was really hammering along. They weren't going to let us get back because we were the great enemy.

"We did eventually get back to the others but we'd had to give everything we had for 80 kilometers. But when we got back up to them, Jef gestured to me that he was fresh enough to attack again, so I could go with him. And we attacked. It was a shame but Dierickx and Jan van Ingelgem [sic] came with us. And the five of us rode together to Mariakerke, where the finish was. I won the sprint and Jef Vandaele came second. We couldn't have hoped for better."

The pact was renewed in the national championship, where Vandaele won and Deman came second.

Van Wijnendaele was content with his race, if not with the paltry crowd at the finish. But he faced questions from colleagues and investors. Was this race of his worth holding? The winner in 1914 was a star—Marcel Buysse honored a promise and took part regardless of his French sponsor, Alcyon, which had forbidden its Belgian riders to ride because the roads were too treacherous—but even van Wijnendaele conceded the rest of the field was second rate.

And then just as the organizers hoped Buysse would persuade other stars and their sponsors to join in, the world went to war. And, specifically, Germany went to war against Belgium. German troops wanted to take Paris quickly to eliminate their greatest opposition, the French. Marching through neutral Belgium and across its porous and unprotected border with France was their way of doing it.

The Germans forcefully asked for right of passage on August 2, 1914. Brussels said no on August 3. And Germany invaded regardless on August 4. The Belgian army, a tenth the size of the invaders, held the Germans back for a month. It must have regretted its bravery: Germany took revenge by executing 6,000 civilians and setting fire to towns. It deported 120,000 men to work in factories in Germany. It was a terrible time and Belgians paid with their blood and flesh for defending their homes.

The war swept on south. German troops came close to capturing the French capital before being beaten back—by troops carried to the Front in Parisian taxis commandeered to circumvent railroads destroyed by the Germans. And then the war came to a halt. The fighting continued but the battles came to a halt. Years of trench warfare followed.

Most people in Belgium, of course, were perplexed. There was no experience of occupation, no army to bring it to an end. Allied resistance was largely in the hands of others. Some resisted nevertheless. Among them was Paul Deman, winner of that first Ronde. He was born in Rekkem, a few kilometers from the French border, in 1889. In the war, he joined the fledgling Resistance and cycled into neutral Holland with documents to send on to the Allies. The Germans finally caught him and put him in jail in Leuven, ready for execution. He would have been shot had the Armistice not saved him.

The story has grown into legend and it's hard to decide how much is true. Did he really carry messages in a gold tooth and, if he did, how would he have done it? And was he really arrested on his 13th and unluckiest mission? Was his execution really due on the very day of the Armistice? Did he twice escape the execution squad? Did Allied soldiers really mistake his West Flemish accent and believe he was German? Any one of those could be true. Some must be because the French awarded him the Croix de Guerre. But the whole collection veers towards romanticizing, don't you think?

Anyway, Deman began training again when the armistice brought peace and he won Paris–Roubaix in 1920. When he retired, it was to work in a small bike shop near the Kluisberg hill that's now a feature of the modern Ronde. His youthful customers included Marc Demeyer, who won Paris–Roubaix in 1976.

Deman lived until July 31, 1961, in time for the Ronde he won to be more important to Belgium than the world championship. He lies now—along with Demeyer and 14 Commonwealth soldiers—in the churchyard at Outrijve, on the banks of the Schelder near Avelgem. It was to there that he moved on retirement, built a villa, surrounded it by a green-painted fence and a neat garden, and bought a bike shop.

Sportwereld closed during the war. Or, at any rate, it was replaced by a more general newspaper, *De Telegraaf*. And then, in 1919, it appeared again and grew to 200,000 copies a day in the 1920s. Van Wijnendaele became its joint owner in 1925. He was the king of Belgian cycling.

Sportwereld may have closed but there *was* a Ronde during the war. If only in name. And not on the road. The spirit—if not the practice—was kept alive by a 150 kilometer race for 26 riders on the track at Evergem, on August 22, 1915. The winner was Leon Buysse, ahead of Oskar Goetgebuer and Albert Desmedt, after four and a half hours. It was never repeated. This battle of unknowns—Buysse had won the Championship of Flanders in 1911 but nothing was ever heard again of Goetgebuer or Desmedt—was nothing as a race, although it did turn out to have a significance in what happened when a second world war enveloped Belgium. And we'll come to that in another 25 years.

The Ronde returned to the road in 1919. Along with one of its oddest tales. Achiel van den Broeck, a sports journalist who spent almost half a century beside van Wijnendaele at *Sportwereld*, said of that race: "The Ronde was won by one of the prototypes of the Flandrians. Ritten [a familiar form of Henri, pronounced *Ritta*] van Lerberghe came straight from the Front, from his military post. He didn't have a bike. He borrowed one from the brother-in-law of another rider, Jules Messelis. And at the start he shouted at everyone, 'I'll ride you all into ground' [*k zal gulder allemaal doodriën*]."

The favorite was Jules van Hevel, winner that year of the Championship of Flanders. He was a lean-faced 24-year-old with a broad mouth and the usual mustache and sad expression. He had turned professional only with the return of peace. After running messages as a trench cyclist, he had joined the mortar brigade, was injured and sent to England for treatment. And hearing this outburst at the start of the Ronde van Vlaanderen, he laughed in van Lerberghe's face. This noisy man may have come second to Marcel Buysse in the 1914 Ronde and only a broken pedal may have kept him from finishing with the leaders in 1913. But that was a world war ago and he had scarcely ridden since. Van Hevel faced no challenge. And he told van Lerberghe so.

Pride was hurt. Nerves were taut. A row began.

"Don't you laugh," van Lerberghe snapped back. "I'll ride you off my wheel right in front of your house." And that is exactly what he did. He

Henri van Lerberghe: "Come back tomorrow, I've got half a day's lead!"

responded to an attack by a Dutchman, Frits Wiersma, with a shout of "Hang on—I'll give you a hand" and then rode away from him some while later at Vichte. He pressed on alone with 120 kilometers to go, most of it against the wind. Behind him, the others admired his theatrics more than his chances and they waited too long before taking him seriously and starting to chase. They'd seen it all before: van Lerberghe had made so many long and often self-destructive breakaways that he was known in the sport and its newspapers as the Death Rider.

Drama then turned to trickery and finally to eccentricity. Van Lerberghe began to grow weak and hungry. He saw a helper beside the road with a bag of food. It was intended for Marcel Buysse. It took only a little talking to persuade the helper that Buysse had dropped out of the race and that it would be a shame to let the food go to waste.

You can only admire the gullibility of Buysse's helper, can't you? Not to mention how he accounted for himself when Buysse appeared some minutes later. But whatever happened later, the reality now was that van Lerberghe had another man's food in his stomach and he was on his way again.

The story now becomes still more preposterous—and it will shortly get simply ridiculous. Van Lerberghe was in full flight when a train halted by a signal came to a stop across the road. In front of him. Legend says van Lerberghe climbed into one of the cars, pushed himself and his bike past a compartment of passengers too astonished to protest, then opened the door on the other side of the train, dropped down to the track, climbed over the crossing barrier and carried on racing. Maybe, less dramatically but every bit as inconveniently, he crawled under the train. Or maybe he squeezed between the cars and just clambered across the couplings. But, however he did it, he didn't wait for the barriers to open or the train to move on.

And you have to remember not only that "legend says" with which the story started but also that it's probable that no reporters were there at the time and that they made the story up, or at any rate enhanced it. And if they didn't do that, well, word of mouth has done it for them since.

Whatever the truth, he reached the finish with more than 14 minutes' lead, the largest margin in Ronde history. But nobody knows just how much lead he had coming into town—it may have been as much as 20 minutes—because, as Achiel van den Broeck recounted: "He reached the finish track at Gentbrugge but, instead riding on to the velodrome, he rode into a café and, as though it was the most ordinary thing in the world, he ordered a beer. And then he had another one. And finally when the track director, Oscar van Braeckel, heard that Ritten was in the bar, he sent his soigneur to get him out and get him on to the track.

And when Ritten rode his lap of honor, he turned to the crowd and he shouted—and this is historical fact, not a joke—"Everyone go home and come back tomorrow! I've got half a day's lead on the others."

"Rode" his lap of honor is perhaps an exaggeration, according to the story. There are pictures of the soigneur steadying him as he walks, certainly. Van Lerberghe is wearing a baggy shirt with laden pockets, a tire round his shoulders and a cap. His soigneur wears a cap, too, his pants held up by suspenders, and what looks like a cape on one shoulder. The unfenced track is lined with people and the two men appear to have walked some way because there is no gap in the crowd through which they could have passed to get on to the track.

Van Lerberghe was a quarter of an hour ahead of the rest, enough to time his lead by the clock on a church tower. But how much he'd drunk and how much his eccentricity was fueled by alcohol is less certain. How many beers could he have downed in that time, knowing the others were now chasing? Would he have drunk enough to be pie-eyed? Did someone have to go into the bar to find him? And could he have drunk enough in a few minutes to need help staying upright?

It would be nice to think it all happened. But the historian, Fer Schroeders, says the story was invented by Achiel Buysse in the 1950s. It is fiction, he says. Even the track director's name varies, from the Oscar van Braeckel in most accounts to Oscar van Braeckman in a history by Rik Vanwalleghem.

But Vanwalleghem and Schroeders do agree. Vanwalleghem says cautiously: "The story doesn't quite chime with the truth. Ritten had a 14-minute lead but the story is a good example of how an anecdote can be repeated in the Press and take on a life of its own, systematically exaggerated. The words that Ritten spoke at the finish seem authentic, but the story of the *demi* of beer was dreamed up by Achiel Buysse, who spun it in the 1950s when he worked for *Het Nieuwsblad*. And ever since this juicy tale has run and run."

The revival of Flanders and its Flandrians demanded bigger and better legends. So did the sales of newspapers. And where the legends didn't exist, they were simply invented. Briek Schotte, a crouched, pinch-faced man who came to typify a later generation of iron-hard men from Flanders, remembered: "Every day, people came up to me to tell me what they remembered my doing, and where I'd done it, things

I'd never done and places I'd never been. They were convinced that my strength came from eating raw meat and drinking brown beer with an egg in it. Which was nonsense."

Nevertheless, van Lerberghe won the Ronde by more than any man has ever won it and, if you go to Lichtervelde , you'll find a plaque in his memory. It says "Here lived Henri 'Ritten' van Lerberghe", followed by details of the race, his winning margin and the dates of his birth and death. In 2004 Lichtervelde was named "village of the race" by the Ronde and a railroad car was parked by the road in the main square in symbolic memory. Van Lerberghe lived all his life in the village until he died at 75 on April 10, 1966.

You were a Flandrian because that was how you were brought up. I knew what that meant, the value of a single centime, of a potato. The bike was a way we could improve ourselves. We put a lot into it and we fought until we could see something for it. Our life depended on it. You don't get the will to fight from having enough or even too much from the time you were a kid. Maybe we were the last generation in the rich West to live like that.

—Briek Schotte

3

Koppen And Bergen

For a small city, Brussels has an extensive rail network. Its map is the usual web of lines going in no consistent order, each a different color. The most striking, because it's colored red, is line 1a. It starts—or ends—in the southwest of the city, runs northeast to the center or downtown region, crosses it and then dives down and to the right.

It has, for a cyclist, two novelties. The first is that the second station when you start in the southwest is named after Eddy Merckx. He is the official Famous Belgian; it was he who was presented when the American secretary of state, Condoleeza Rice, visited the city in 2005 and asked to meet a Famous Belgian. A joke at the time suggested there weren't any. But Merckx had won an unsurpassed five Tours de France and so many other races that he suppressed riders' wages and sponsors' interest for a decade. He was at the same time a wave of national pride and a cold shower on the prosperity of the sport. Who wanted to support a team if Merckx wasn't in it? What was left for lesser riders once organizers had paid out most of what they had to be sure the great man was in their race?

The other station of significance is seven stops further on, between Aumale and the city's western rail terminus. It is named after Jacques Brel. And this may take some explaining.

Jacques Brel was a fleshy-lipped singer with an aptitude for sweating profusely on stage. He wrote and sang powerful ballads in French, but sometimes in Dutch, and remains to this day the best-loved singer in Belgium and one of the most respected throughout the French-speaking world. His was a short life. He didn't live to make 50. After selling more than 25 million records, he set off to sail round the world in a 19-meter yacht. On the way he was diagnosed with cancer. It came as no surprise: he had smoked heavily and he had already written his will. He died of cancer when he was 49.

All this is worth mentioning for the one song, *Mon Plat Pays*, which has become a folk anthem. The title means "my flat country", and the song tells of a featureless land that runs level into a featureless sea, playing on the French word *vague* which means both "wave" and "indistinct." And Belgium, at any rate Flemish Belgium, is indeed flat. It just fades into the North Sea. It's a country of modern towns surrounded by small pastures, by rows of poplars lining long straight drainage ditches, and by villages named as often as not after a saint or church. Flanders, through its smallness, is philosophically little more than a village.

And yet there *are* hills. Not long, not high but always steep. And with clumsy, consonant-laden names which nevertheless sound like poetry: Koppenberg, Kluisberg, Kruisberg, Knokteberg, Steenbeekberg. They have the scent of faraway places with strange-sounding names, the diphthong of *ui* in Dutch not obvious to English speakers, nor the half-breathiness, half-fricative of the Belgian G. And the closeness to the French border shows because, when the hills don't end in -*berg*, they end instead in -*mont*. Together, they sound less like geography than a witch's incantation.

They are, nearly all, the product of some improbable geological eruption, in an arc south of Oudenaarde. They have been there for millions of years, strange, bad-tempered acne on the landscape of the *plat pays*, but they weren't in the first Tours of Flanders. Stories from 1913 and 1914 don't mention hills anywhere. And then in 1919 they appeared. The race still rode a different route each year—only in 1947 did a pattern emerge—and in 1919 it took in the Tiegemberg and the Kwaremont. They remained the only hills until 1930, although the Kruisberg appeared in 1928 only to be dropped the following year.

Their cobbles are a relic of the days when teams like Alcyon considered Belgium too dangerous for their riders. It's easy to forget just how recent asphalt is: it was first used, in blocks, in the Champs Elysées only in 1824 and it wasn't brought to its modern standard until 1872. There's an irony in that while modern asphalt was developed by a Belgian immigrant to the USA, Edward de Smedt, his home country was one of the slowest in western Europe to adopt it. Belgian roads in the first half of the 20th century were in a poor state, few of them surfaced or, when they *were* surfaced, covered in rough and unmaintained cobbles.

For the most part, roads connecting cities were just compressed ash. They've gone now, of course, but history lingers. Take a look at the name of the biggest roads and often you'll read *steenweg*. The town of Turnhout has the Antwerpsesteenweg running to Antwerp in the west and then the Steenweg op Gierle and the Steenweg op Diest and the Steenweg op Mol and plenty of others running like spokes from a hub. *Steenweg* means "stone road". A road that was covered in stone rather than ash was remarkable enough to boast of it in its name.

But they came, nearly all of them, after the start of the Ronde. Rik Vanwalleghem calls the roads of those first races "pre-historic." And then in 1920 van Wijnendaele added the stretch along the coast to Oostend that was to stay for another 18 years. To him, the flat and then unbuilt land behind the dunes of the North Sea defined Flanders as it did later for Jacques Brel. And there was always a good chance the wind would sweep across the struggling bunch and make lives still more miserable.

Planning a route like that was no trouble. Van Wijnendaele just got out a map and drew lines where he wanted to go. There was too little other traffic for the road to be closed as the race passed and there were too few riders to need it. There were never more than 50 participants before 1920. It wasn't until 1931 that there were more than 100. And they were soon broken into groups by the wind, the hills and the road. The traffic was the least of their problems.

Where they could, riders struggled on the cobbles or on broken stones. But often they couldn't and they strung out instead on the impromptu and narrow ash cycle paths that ran on the road's edge. Those were smoother but there was no telling what was hidden in their soft soot and the risk of a flat tire was greater. And the chance of a crash, too, because riders in a long line had to stay closer to the wheel in front to avoid the wind, and the erratic surface—it could change from compact dust and gravel to something softer and wheel-sucking or perhaps to barely hidden rocks—made a touched wheel and a fall a constant risk. And it wasn't unknown for ambitious riders to try to overtake on even the narrowest paths, elbowing rivals out of the way.

"The worst roads now are better than the best roads then," says Rik Vanwalleghem.

This could have tragic-comic consequences. Gustaf van Slembrouck, not the least colorful of riders, crashed on one such path as riders struggled for the best position. A cow grazing beside the road had panicked and backed into him. Legend says that, his chance of winning gone but his opportunities for clowning increased, he stood up, plucked the bottle from his bike, advanced on the cow—and began milking it.

As with many of these stories, it is slightly too good to be true. But it's possible, at least, that he pretended to milk the cow, because he was an easygoing, laughing man who delighted at having his picture taken. If you ever see a staged photo of riders at the front of a race sharing a cigarette, one of them is van Slembrouck. He's the one on the right, giving a light to Maurice Geldhof in the Tour of 1927. Not just a clown, by the way: van Slembrouck was a handsome man with a strong face and bright eyes and a film star's smile who led the Tour de France for seven days in 1926, and won four stages over his career. And he came second in the Ronde in 1926 and 1927. He was as aggressive in races as he was friendly out of them, but a poor sense of tactics denied him greater success. He retired to Oostend, the port where he was born, and started a bike factory. He died in the town in July 1968.

But you want a story from that era that *is* true? Well, the 1926 race was a particularly hectic one, with attack after attack. Ten riders got to the end together and around half of them fell off. Denis Verschueren sprinted through the confusion, beating van Slembrouck and Raymond Decorte and won the Ronde—in his first race as a professional. And the first in the Ronde to better 30 kilometers per hour.

The hills now make the race. But they had their first serious effect as far back as 1921. There were still only the Kwaremont and the Tiegemberg but the first was enough to blow apart those of the 90 starters who had got that far. The Ronde had been up the hill the previous year but not then with the same devastating effect. In 1921 it split the field into individuals struggling just to get up, a dozen of whom managed to group.

And that dozen didn't last long because eight fell by the wayside in a handful of kilometers. Jules van Hevel, whom we met earlier, was there in the leading contingent. He'd won the previous spring and was therefore the favorite. With him was the curly-haired René Vermandel, the

Jules van Hevel: straight out of the trenches to ride the Ronde on a borrowed bike.

experienced but largely unsuccessful Berten De Jonghe, and a French-speaking southern Belgian called Louis Mottiat.

Van Wijnendaele wrote: "As they came on to the track at Gentbrugge, Berten Dejonghe was leading, with van Hevel on his wheel. It was clear that Dejonghe wanted to lead out the sprint for his training partner. With another circuit of the track—400 meters—Dejonghe is still at the front. Another 300 meters. Van Hevel, looking quickly to the right, can't see Vermandel, who he thinks has pulled his foot out of his pedal.

He shouts at Dejonghe to let him get past. Berten swung over to the left, therefore, and opened the way for Dejonghe…but with Vermandel on his wheel.

"Perfectly aware of Jules van Hevel's tactics, the crafty René had taken care to hide on the left. And 50 meters from the line, perfectly sucked along by his improvised 'Derny', Vermandel had only to go round van Hevel to win by half a length!"

The Ronde's long struggle for international respectability finally succeeded in 1922. It was cold and misty that morning of Sunday, March 19, no day to be out on your bike. But there on the line among the 91 starters were Henri and Francis Pélissier. It was a great coup for van Wijnendaele.

The Frenchmen's significance in international cycling, particularly Henri's, has faded now. Spectators driving into the track in Vincennes in western Paris where the Tour de France ended before it moved to the Champs Elysées don't even look up as they pass a bas-relief of the three Pélissiers—there was another brother, Charles—but at the time they were the world's two most glamorous riders.

Henri, for instance, won the Tour of Lombardy in 1911 and again in 1913, after which he had had to hide in a watchtower and await the arrival of police to save him from Italian fans angry that he had beaten their favorite, Costante Girardengo. Henri also won Milan–San Remo in 1912 and Bordeaux–Paris in 1919 and Paris–Roubaix in 1919 and 1921.

Henri was a stunning rider but a difficult man, a cantankerous amateur lawyer who fought repeatedly with Henri Desgrange and anyone else who offended him, as it seems most people did. Desgrange called him "a pig-headedly arrogant champion" and said: "He treated every organizer and every sponsor as an enemy."

The row between the two Henris, each as pig-headed as the other, came to a head in the Tour de France in 1924 when Desgrange insisted riders end the day with no fewer clothes than those in which they'd started. Stages in those days started before dawn but Desgrange insisted riders couldn't seek relief from the afternoon sun by taking off the jerseys they'd needed in the cold of night. Henri had taken off one of his and thrown it on the road in protest. Desgrange demanded he pick it up and put it back on. Pélissier refused. The row grew more heated and ended only when Henri and Francis walked out of the race and sat and sulked in a café at Coutances train station and told a journalist, Albert Londres, lurid and exaggerated tales of drug-taking.

No good came of it, other than for Londres, who had an exclusive. Henri Pélissier's first wife despaired of him and committed suicide. He took a lover 20 years younger who fared little better. But instead of shooting herself, she shot Pélissier with the same gun.

The Pélissier brothers made the Ronde a sensation in 1922 even though Francis, the younger, came third to Léon Devos and Henri

Henri and Francis Pélissier: Henri was murdered and Francis became a team boss.

came only fourth. Those numbers, though, hide the story. Because Devos—"the fox" in Dutch—won by 7 minutes 40 seconds from a further Frenchman, Jean Brunier, and no less than 27 minutes 43 seconds on the two Pélissiers. He broke away in the hills and rode 120 kilometers by himself, chased but never caught by Brunier. A race in which the mighty Pélissier brothers could be so humbled made the cycling world sit up.

The story spread, of course. So, no doubt, did the tale of how the bell had been rung a lap too early on the track at the finish and that everyone from fifth to twenty-first had to be placed equal. But heroism and grit were the real tale, and the race was suddenly worthy of international attention.

Next year Heiri Suter of Switzerland became the first foreigner to win. Although it was a mixed blessing. Folk rang their bells in delight in the green mountain valleys of Helvetia, no doubt, but as the American writer, Gabé Konrad, said: "Suter's victory angered the organizers

Heiri Suter, the Ronde's first foreign winner.

not only because he was a foreigner, but also because of his style of cycling. He was a thinking man's rider, relying on interval training and tactics to see him to the line rather than the brute force of riding everyone off your wheel that Belgians fans were so accustomed to." He was, in other words, too scientific, too dull.

And nor was that the only change on the way. There were 84 starters that spring. By 1933, after word had spread, there were 164. The Ronde had come of age.

A Flandrian gives everything he's got, the whole day. He holds nothing back. He doesn't count the effort. He is someone with extraordinary willpower.

—Marc Sergeant

4

Riding For The Money

Henri Desgrange invented a sport—multi-day road cycling. There had been nothing like the Tour de France because it was he who created it. And the rules that he wrote, his draconian style of enforcing them, and the ethos that he created spread through the sport. To Desgrange, cycling was incidental. He wanted a race between men, a race so hard that only one would have the strength to finish. That finisher would be a superman to inspire the nation. He wanted a better world. He wanted to correct the under-development, the under-nourishment and the lack of health in French youth which he believed had lost the Franco-Prussian war and led so many to be rejected as soldiers during world war one. Sport was the way to inspire the young and make them strong to save the nation. His campaigning went as far as publicly shaming riders he saw leaving the Parc des Princes track without taking a shower. He called his column *Pieds Sales*—"Dirty Feet."

And to achieve that, he made cycling as hard as he could, not just with mountains but a succession of petty rules of the sort that led the Pélissier brothers to go on strike.

The Ronde didn't have that crusading mentality but it was of that same era. Riders were to be self-sufficient, to the extent of not cooperating even with those in the same team. But society changed and the rules of cycling with it, slowly admittedly but faster in the Ronde than in the Tour. Riders in the 1930s were still expected to ride with spare tires and a pump. They could switch to another bike if they broke a frame, wheel or their handlebars but otherwise they were to make their own repairs. With permission, they could accept further spare tires or a pump, or put on a rain jacket, but only in an emergency.

Prizes in the Ronde grew but not enormously. When Frans Bonduel won in 1930 he collected 2,000 francs as first prize and then 2,000 as a bonus from his sponsor, the Dilecta bike company. Dilecta, incidentally, was founded in 1912 by a man called Albert Chichery. He had seen his destiny in life as cutting up meat and selling it. But then he watched a bike race in the town of Le Blanc, in the French *département* of Indre where he lived, and he thought he'd have a go at racing instead. Like van Wijnendaele, though, he had more ambition than talent and soon realized that he'd be better off in business. Clearly not lacking for money, he bought the bike factory in the town. And there he prospered. There are several explanations for his death, although the fact that he had a single bullet in his head isn't disputed. The most colorful story is that his politics didn't suit the Resistance.

Anyway, to get back to the prizes, Bonduel collected 4,000 francs for winning the biggest race in Flanders. As a reference, a newspaper in those days cost 40 centimes. As a better reference, Fer Schroeders says a house cost 50,000 francs in 1930. That would depend on what house and where, of course. But, as he said: "To make a fortune in cycling, you had to win a lot of big races…"

By 1935 the prizes amounted to 12,500 francs, with 2,500 for the winner down to 125 for 19th. In 1938 there was a bonus of 100 francs for any rider who led by 30 minutes.

Good riders made more from small races than from big ones, though. It wasn't because the prizes were better but because the competition was less and because in purely local races they were paid to ride. Cinema newsreels brought distant races into small towns and pushed up the value of stars. Few people traveled and for most the only time they saw riders from outside their region was at the cinema or when stars could be paid to ride some local round-the-houses race.

These races brought a newsreel to life. And brought newspaper stories to life. Because, as the Dutch writer Benjamin Maso has pointed out, journalists, publishers and riders contrived to make cycling a legend more than a sport. Tales were told that could not be told with the arrival of radio and then television. If glamor and bravery lacked, then glamor and bravery could be added, inconvenient facts and scandals hidden. And they were, in the Ronde but even more in big stage races such as the Tour de France.

Seeing the gods of a sport riding the very roads on which you made your daily bike trudge to work was worth the cost of admission. You could look forward to it for weeks, discuss it with your pals before and afterwards, join the scramble for autographs. And the better the stars, the more who paid to watch and the better the contracts could be. The tradition lasted 50 years, with most riders in the Tour de France wanting no more than to finish and increase their value for appearances to follow. Where Lucien Petit-Breton rode 30 races a year at the start of the century, Fausto Coppi and Gino Bartali rode 60 in the 1950s, Jacques Anquetil 85 in the sixties and Eddy Merckx 150 in the seventies. After 1980, riders' salaries and bonuses improved to the point that they no longer needed these rides and, if asked to take part, demanded more than most could afford.

Briek Schotte said most professionals received little more than a bike and tires and a jersey. The rest they had to sort out for themselves. Wim van Est said the same, adding that he got just one jersey and, if he fell and tore it, had to pay a fine for riding in another one. The point of turning professional was rarely the salary: it was that there was more money to win, more money from appearance contracts. And that made races more individual.

Schotte recalled: "The Ronde before and after the war was more attractive and more spectacular than it is now. Team tactics didn't exist then. It was everyone for himself. Everyone rode for the prizes, and for the primes, which in those days were the only income a rider had. In my first Ronde I earned 2,000 francs. And as third overall I got 1,500 francs. As the first to the top of the Edelare, I got another 500. That was a whole lot of money in 1940. The hourly wage would have been around 4 francs. And there were a lot of prizes in kind. I remember one day my mother said to me where she washed clothes, 'Am I expected to spend all my life with my hands in this sink?', and I said, 'Hang on, I'm going to get a washing machine out of the Ronde van Vlaanderen.' And I did, too."

SCHOTTE'S TEN GOLDEN RULES
   1: Be happy with what you've got
   2: Determination and patience get you everywhere
   3: Tired? If you're tired, go to bed

4: Never lose your freedom

5: Stay who you are

6: Watch and you'll learn a lot

7: Let yourself go and you lose yourself

8: Never forget your roots

9: Never believe in dreams you can't make come true

10: Speak ill and ill will come of you

The growing status of the race and the increasing talent of those taking part brought problems. Crowds became a hazard on roads unclosed to other traffic. They became, as one writer colorfully put it, like a blood clot about to burst.

Stijn Streuvels wrote to *Sportwereld* in 1937 that the Ronde as seen from *Het Lijsternest* ("the thrush's nest"), his house in Ingooigem, was "more a procession of cars than of riders." Rik Vanwalleghem wrote of a "wild rodeo" of drivers following the race and looking for short cuts to see the riders several times. The police estimated the crowd for early races at 500,000. Fans stood so thick at control points, where riders signed a log to prove they had stuck to the route, that the race had trouble passing. The event was on public roads and public roads were for everyone. And everyone, it seemed, made the most of them. The Ronde had no security organization to counter it, nor the power to do so. The 1937 race was so chaotic that van Wijnendaele wrote on March 30, 1938: "To control as far as possible the plague of race-followers and assure the dependable running of our races, we have sent an exceptional request to the roads ministry to have our race followed by several gendarmes on motorbikes.... They will have the right to penalize anybody following the race without permission."

The last and oddest victory before the war—well, second oddest, really, since nothing is going to beat van Lerberghe—belonged to Karel Kaers in 1939. The youngest man to have won the world road champion-ship—in 1934, when he was 20—was training for Paris-Roubaix. He wanted a hard Ronde but not a long one, so he drove to the Kware-mont, locked his car and rode for an hour and a half into Gent and the start. All he had to do was to ride as far as the Kwaremont, get off his bike with some feigned excuse, then drive home. It would suit him to limit the number of hills he had to go up because he was hefty—85 kilograms (187 pounds)—and many had criticized him as an unworthy world champion because the course, near Leipzig in Germany, had been flat and undemanding.

Well, the race started and he felt good and, knowing he wasn't going the whole distance, he broke clear just before the Kwaremont, with Roger van den Driessche. Kaers then realized that he had a minute's

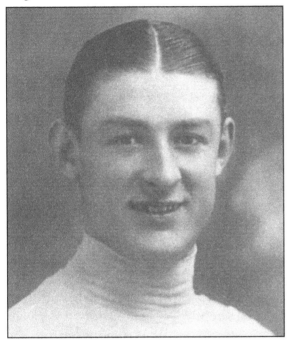

Karel Kaers, the youngest world champion and inadvertent winner of the Ronde.

lead and a good chance of winning in a sprint if he could just grit his teeth enough on the climbs. He couldn't just get to the top of the Kwaremont, climb off his bike and put it into the car.

But he didn't need to: his manager had gotten wind of the plan and had driven off in the car. So Kaers just pressed on instead and won the race. It was the last before the world went back to war. Kaers raced for the last time in May 1948, on the track at Ordrup, near Copenhagen. He retired to run a bar set into the entrance of the *Sportpaleis*, a whale-like barn of a track, now demolished, on the outskirts of Antwerp in Merksem. It was in an ugly brick building, beside the road north to Holland and within signposting distance of the docks. The car park was large and unkempt enough to pass for a half-cleared bombsite. The outside of the building used to have an advertisement painted on the brick for a communist newspaper that had gone out of business years earlier. The track was so large that six-days there were raced by teams of three rather than two and it became so cold in the evening that riders wore warmup tops.

"There's a lot of beer sold in that pub when the fans pour out of a big meeting," the Franco-American journalist René de Latour wrote in *Sporting Cyclist*. "Each time a new barrel is started, the owner himself has to test the quality of the beer, and these frequent tests have made the man concerned a bit thick on the hips. It is hard to remember that this man was once a splendid athlete."

Kaers died in December 1972, when he was 58.

By now, van Wijnendaele's life had advanced with his race. He became joint owner of his paper in 1925 and, after the death of Leon van den Haute in 1931, its sole owner. But he wrote better than he managed money. *Sportwereld* had to be sold. It became part of the Standaard group and remains to this day a section of *Het Nieuwsblad*, a general paper first published in 1918. *Het Nieuwsblad* therefore organizes the Ronde. But in that circular way of history, it also organizes the race set up as its rival after the war—a race created because van Wijnendaele and the Ronde van Vlaanderen were accused of collaborating with the Germans.

German troops occupied Belgium in May 1940. Belgium again resisted but it crumbled, as all the invaded nations of western Europe crumbled, to the force of German troops coming in from the north and east. The government escaped to London, leaving the king, Leopold III, to be held under house arrest.

Collaboration wasn't rife but it wasn't unknown. At its severest, Walloons in the south joined a German army infantry battalion, the 373rd, and fought in Russia. Flemish collaborators in the north were recruited into the SS. That difference has troubled older Belgians ever since and a French-language song in the 1970s caused great controversy when it accused the Flemish of being too Germanic to resist.

The tensions and differences remain. In 2007, a 1,114-page historical study of the war listed the ways in which Belgian authorities followed and sometimes exceeded the demands of the Germans in segregating, robbing and rounding up Jews. French-language newspapers gave the report a lot more coverage than their counterparts in the north, which one report said barely mentioned it or kept it on inside pages. It didn't help that in 2011 the extreme-right *Vlaamse Belang* (Flanders' Interests) party demanded an amnesty for wartime collaborators.

Het Nieuwsblad changed its name during the war to *Het Algemeen Nieuws-Sportwereld*, and many said it was a mouthpiece for the occupiers. It certainly continued to organize the Ronde, which was the only classic held on German-occupied territory. Van Wijnendaele had heard that Liège–Bastogne–Liège had also asked for German permission to continue. His Flemish pride then obliged him to seek permission as well—permission he got but without the knowledge that his French-speaking neighbors had since changed their mind and wouldn't be organizing a race after all.

It's impossible to know now what went through van Wijnendaele's mind when he *did* find out. How much did he debate the advantage his race would get in carrying on where its older rival hadn't; how much did he think it was simply in Flanders' interest to have something in those dark days in which it could continue to be proud; and how much did he worry that he was collaborating with the occupier?

What we *do* know is that he said in his announcement of the 1941 race that it could be run thanks to "the permission of the occupiers." The Germans, says Gabe Konrad, then "not only allowed and enjoyed the race but helped police the route as well." Only Belgians took part because foreigners were banned from crossing the border.

The collaboration led *De Standaard* and *Het Algemeen Nieuws-Sportwereld* to be sequestered by the state when peace returned—the same fate that came to *L'Auto*, organizer of the Tour de France.

Several of the Belgian paper's journalists, although largely not the sports reporters, were punished as collaborators. One of them, Achiel van den Broeck, argued that he'd never have written anything to oblige the Germans but that reporting the life of cyclists did nothing to prolong the occupation. The plea fell flat. He and van Wijnendaele were banned from journalism for the rest of their lives, for organizing the Ronde and for writing about it. In effect, the race was confiscated. And again legend provides a sequel, because it insists that van Wijnendaele's ban was lifted after the British general, Bernard Montgomery, wrote to confirm that van Wijnendaele had hidden a British pilot in his house so that he could be handed to escape lines.

Montgomery's papers are in the Imperial War Museum in London. There is no mention in the collection index of a letter or anything else about downed pilots. And nothing about van Wijnendaele. Which isn't to say that the letter was never written—it may be in the family's ownership or in a museum in Belgium—but it hasn't been reproduced. And the story doesn't explain how a man in occupied Belgium might know the operational commander of D-Day and the general who defeated Rommel in north Africa, nor why an army general would know of individual RAF pilots and where they were sheltered. Since the point of escape lines and safe houses was secrecy, why would they be familiar to foreigners?

Whatever the truth, van Wijnendaele's sentence was lifted in 1948. In 1952 he received the freedom of Torhout and he was made a knight, the lowest class of the Order of Leopold.

His troubles didn't end immediately, however. His race now had a rival, the Omloop Het Volk, named after a daily paper started in 1891 by Christian labor organizations opposed to socialism. It, too, continued to publish during the war but it stayed more distant from the Germans. That gave it a chance to feel superior and to capitalize on its rival's tarnished image and in 1945 it began its own race, the *Omloop* van Vlaanderen. It organized it just two weeks before the *Ronde* van Vlaanderen and the intention was clear: it was a spoiler for the older race and potentially a substitute for it.

Van Wijnendaele was not happy. He complained first to his tormentors, who refused to budge. Then he went to the national cycling federation, and then he went to the law. The legal battle lasted a year, one side claiming the other's name was too close to be fair, the other insisting it wasn't. In the end *Het Volk* was reminded pointedly that *Omloop* and *Ronde* meant much the same thing in Dutch and that *Het Volk* must rename its race. And so it became the Omloop Het Volk.

The Omloop thrived better than its owners. The race never achieved the classic status of the Ronde, a point of irritation for the paper's owners when in the 1980s the world body, the UCI, tried to have a classic in each of the largest countries in its membership—and included some doubtful and short-lived races, including in Britain. And the newspaper fared still less well. It had its offices in Forelstraat, a mixed street of houses, offices, shops and churches in south-east

Gent. But Belgium is small and Dutch-speaking Flanders even smaller. There wasn't room for all who wanted to sell papers. *Het Volk* was sold in 1994 to the *Vlaamse Uitgeversmaatschappij*—the Flemish Publishing Company, now known as Corelio—which also published *De Standaard*, the heavyweight paper in Brussels, and *Het Nieuwsblad*, a more general and popular paper. By 2001 *Het Volk* and its new sisters became indistinguishable, sharing journalists and an editor, and eventually it had no more than a different front page. The paper moved from Gent to near Brussels in 2000 and went out of business in May 2008 after 117 years. The race is now called the Omloop Het Nieuwsblad, although it will be a long time before cycling fans stop referring to it by habit as the Omloop Het Volk.

Equipment was scarce during the war. The Ronde banned derailleurs, to make everyone equal. Schotte won the 1942 Ronde on a gear of 49 x 17, which he acknowledged that a decade or two later was no more than a training gear. But he still averaged better than 34 kilometers per hour. Prizes were whatever the organizers could find. Riders received boxes of razors, bottles of wine and cycling equipment. Many took anything, knowing they could sell it for inflated prices on the black market. Sometimes, when the prize was bulky and there was neither transport nor gasoline to deliver it, riders had to collect it themselves.

Among those who mastered the black market early was a man who throughout his career had an extraordinary taste for money: Rik van Steenbergen. As a rider he sometimes signed for three races in a day, collecting his start money, riding a third of the distance to justify his contract and then driving to the next. He once refused to start at the Herne Hill track in London until he'd been paid, and in cash. *Cycling* remembered: "With the crowd growing impatient, the promoter had to do a fast whip-round of the turnstiles and empty his own wallet before van Steenbergen consented to take to the track."

Van Steenbergen is the Ronde's youngest winner: he was 19 years and 204 days old on April 2, 1944. That made him still a junior, too young to turn professional. The trick was done with a forged German identity card. He was 15 when Germany invaded Belgium, one of a family so poor they could eat little more than bread. Riding a bike was a way of making money and the habit never left him. His family did all it could to stop his riding a bike but, to him and eventually for them, it was a way out of poverty. The memory never left him and it shaped his attitude to money and to his awareness of how short his career might be.

He also entered the Circuit of Flanders when he was too young but the judges dismissed him as a no-hoper and turned a blind eye. What difference could a kid like that make? Much better to let him ride and

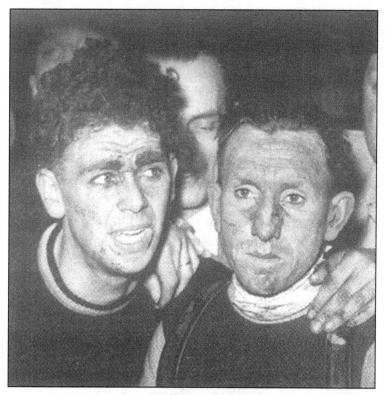

Rik van Steenbergen (left) and Briek Schotte (right), lions of Flanders.

learn a lesson than send him home disappointed. And then van Steenbergen won the hills championship, the time-trial, the final stage and the overall race. After that even he never knew how many races he had ridden or won.

Among races he *did* win were the Ronde in 1944 and 1946. And yet he said: "I won the first two that I rode. Love at first sight, you'd think. But I never thought it was a race for me. It was a love-hate relationship. When I started as a professional in 1943, I wasn't allowed to ride it. In those days there were three classes of rider: Road-riders A, road-riders B and track riders. I was registered with the federation as a track rider. At first I wasn't allowed to ride the national road championship in 1943. And then on the Wednesday before the race my manager, Jean van Buggenhout, got it together that I could ride. I won and that made me an A-class rider."

And that got him into the 1944 Ronde, which he won from Briek Schotte in a sprint. But that desire for money had already gripped him. "I didn't ride the following year's race because I could probably earn more elsewhere. You have to remember that the Ronde didn't have the glamor that it does now, especially internationally. And as well as that, I was a *Kempenaar* [someone from the Antwerp area] and the Ronde counted for less in the eastern provinces of northern Belgium than in East and West Flanders."

It seems lost now, what he did that Sunday in 1945. But in 1946 he again went to the start in Gent. And this time he won not by centimeters but by a minute and ten seconds. That would be an impressive margin at any time. What makes it more remarkable is that he got that lead only in the last hour.

"It was one of my best wins ever," he said. "I could do whatever I wanted. I thrashed the field to shreds. Towards the end I had just Schotte and Louis Thiétard with me. They were just happy to follow. We came to an agreement. I said they could stay with me as far as Kwatrecht [a village near Wetteren, 10 kilometers southeast of Gent]. If they could help a bit before then, I wouldn't drop them. They were happy with that. They had no choice. And then under the bridge at Kwatrecht, I shot them off."

Did that persuade him to return to the Ronde?

No. He stayed away, again for money.

"In the spring in those years there were still good track races with good riders. Some years I earned more money on the track than on the road. And the weather in the Ronde never suited me."

When he did return, in 1951, there was no comeback of the conquering hero. Fiorenzo Magni won for the third successive season—more of that later—and van Steenbergen finished sixth, "as frozen as an ice cube." He was the sorry best of a Belgian field that had been humiliated on home soil by two Italians and three Frenchmen. The Ronde had become international and Belgium was paying the price.

"I really can't think now what possessed me to ride it," he remembered years afterward. "I must have thought it was good training for Paris–Roubaix. But I never thought of the Ronde as riders think of it now. That year, 1951, the whole field was wrecked by the cold. We all crossed the finish line like ghosts, rotten with cold."

In 1955 he crossed the line not rotten with cold but ruined by anxiety. The winner that day was Louison Bobet but the true story belongs to van Steenbergen. When he moved, everyone moved, and the same went for the Frenchman, Bobet. It was no surprise, then, that van Steenbergen and Bobet and the elegant Swiss, Hugo Koblet, got into a break of dreams on the climb of Kloosterstraat.

Wherever Bobet went, Bernard Gauthier went with him. He was Bobet's man-servant, although less elegant than a butler; he was a photographer's dreams for the agonized faces he pulled throughout races and, especially, in the monster Bordeaux–Paris, which he won in 1951, 1954, 1956 and 1957. Bobet shamelessly made him work for his salary, demanding he shelter him and close the slightest gap opened by the others.

Van Steenbergen wasn't troubled that Bobet had a teammate. Gauthier would be too exhausted to bother him in a sprint and Bobet had the reputation of riding like a postman, as the French put it, meaning that he had one speed and had trouble going faster. He looked at Koblet and remembered that the Swiss was a talented *rouleur*, a man who could ride impressively by himself, but that he was no sprinter.

"In my mind I knew I was the fastest of the four," van Steenbergen said, "and I couldn't see how I could lose. But then at Wichelen we were just getting to the railroad crossing when the barrier came down in front of us. Bobet started climbing over it and so did Koblet and Gauthier. But that was against the law in Belgium, so I hesitated. Finally I didn't have a choice any more. And I climbed over the barrier as well."

The cars following the race waited for the train to pass and then for the barrier to reopen. It was then that the commissaire, the chief official, drove up beside van Steenbergen. Georges Vandekerckhove was an easily recognised figure in Belgian cycling thanks to his thin, severe face and a little mustache. He looked every bit the official you hoped not to find alongside you after a transgression.

"He told me I was disqualified," van Steenbergen said, but he and the others rode on. The moment was curiously like a moment that would befall another Belgian sprinter, Freddy Maertens, 30 years later. We'll come to that later.

"Well, you can imagine how that made my legs feel full of lead. We got to a sprint which I should never have lost and I was just third. A real disappointment."

At some stage, just as with Maertens, the judges changed their mind. Bobet, the postman, won the sprint after being protected all afternoon by Gauthier, Koblet came second and Gauthier finished behind van Steenbergen. It's not clear whether Vandekerckhove spoke only to

Louison Bobet: in his presence you were among cycling's royalty.

van Steenbergen after the railroad crossing or whether he spoke to them all but the others chose not to hear. Or if he spoke in Dutch that the others couldn't understand. In the end the commissaires decided the incident hadn't affected the outcome of the race and perhaps that it would be unreasonable to disqualify riders who had only done in Belgium what they systematically did in their own country and elsewhere.

It's also worth noting that Bobet was visiting royalty. He was a *patron* of cycling, a man whose influence spread throughout the sport and who could demand subservience from others. Sleeping dogs could be allowed to lie.

Van Steenbergen lost the 1956 race through outside influences as well. Except that this time it was one of his supposed helpers in the blue and yellow of the Elvé-Peugeot team. Alex Close, a French-speaking Belgian born in November 1921, turned professional only when he was 27. He soon showed himself an excellent climber, especially in stage races. He had ambitions of winning the Ronde in 1956 because he had won the Tour of Belgium the year before. Perhaps anything was worth that chance.

Van Steenbergen said: "I'd caught Fred De Bruyne and going through Wetteren I started going for it hard. I had a gap. But Close chased after me and closed it again. Well, the team system wasn't then what it is now and everybody rode for his own account. But without Close, I could probably have won."

Those were the words he told reporters long afterwards. It's doubtful whether he was as diplomatic after the race to Close himself. A rider like van Steenbergen, as with Rik van Looy after him, had a lot of influence over who rode where and who could win what. Nobody knows what went on between van Steenbergen and Close and what revenge may have been taken. All we know is that Close won 30 races before 1956 and only one afterwards.

"In the days when I started racing," he told Rik van Looy in an interview on Belgian television, "there were just six races that were really important. And for those, you were prepared by your soigneur. We took drugs only for those six races, not like today. We used to keep it in our pockets and take it when we were 60, perhaps 100, kilometers from the finish. But if we were in a break with perhaps four or five minutes' lead, then the stuff stayed in our pockets and we didn't take anything. That was how it was. Then later there were syringes and this and that and it was all more modern."

Van Steenbergen's farewell race was in December 1966 on the lengthy and cold—there was an ice rink in the middle—indoor track at the Sportpaleis on the edge of Antwerp. Twenty-five thousand people turned up that night to say farewell. And then he put his bike in the car for the last time and drove home.

"When I stopped racing," he said, "I knew nothing. There was nothing for me to do. I had been a racing cyclist. Now there was nothing. I should have stopped slowly, but I didn't. It was very sudden and there was a gap in my life. And I fell into bad company." Whence the stories of drunken nights, shady business deals and mixing with people known to the police. What saved him was December 1970, when he met a woman called Doreen who had been working in Belgium. Being British, she had no idea her new friend had once been the best cyclist in the world. They moved to a Spanish-looking villa at Zoersel in Heathland 10 kilometers east of Antwerp. The house had a tower, set among trees with a swimming pool behind it. The wall of the main room was hung with a color picture of van Steenbergen in his red Solo jersey, from the days when a young Eddy Merckx was a teammate. On the facing wall was a close on life-size picture of van Steenbergen in one of his three rainbow jerseys.

Together, at Christmas, he and Doreen would walk through the shopping crowds of Wigan, where Doreen's parents lived. To the British its name produces a weary smile, helped by ancient jokes about Wigan pier. The jokes, if they were ever that funny, depend on your knowing that Wigan is an unexciting industrial town on the edge of Manchester and well inland. The reference was simply reinforced by George Orwell's book, *The Road to Wigan Pier*.

Van Steenbergen learned respectable English through his friendship and then marriage to Doreen and he enjoyed Wigan because nobody knew him there.

"For 12 years before that I just sat and did nothing," he said, "had no spirit left, really. I think I rode a year or two too long. If I had stopped a bit earlier I would have had more character to do something else. My first wife left. I started going out drinking, having fun, falling in with bad friends. There is a danger in doing that if you keep going out like that. I had been living here all alone and a man by himself—well, you know what I mean. You go out visiting…"

There were stories, which he denied, that he had been to jail. He conceded that those close to him had been less fortunate and that police had questioned him about those friendships. "But, no, I never went to jail. Imagine the fuss that would have caused. *Van Steenbergen in gevangenis!*" He flexed his arms to suggest the width of the headlines his imprisonment would have made.

"The truth is that all sorts of stories circulate about you when you're well known."

What he couldn't have denied, because there was not especially appealing evidence, is that he convincingly acted the role of a fat naked sailor in a Belgian sex film. He died of cancer in May 2003.

The Tour of Flanders was originally two weeks before Easter. But that made a clash with Milan–San Remo. The collision was less important then, it's true, because travel across Europe was so difficult. Riders usually rode whichever race was nearer. Riding abroad was difficult even decades later. Wim van Est traveled just 400 kilometers to the Grand Prix des Nations in Paris, his dismantled bike in the luggage net above his seat in the train. He faced customs controls at the Belgian border and again on entering France and he needed a passport and three different currencies.

The Ronde moved eight days into the year at the start of the 1930s, skipping the clash with the Italians and ending up a week before Paris–Roubaix. That alone created international interest because one race now showed form for the one that followed and gave journalists a lot to talk about.

Then in 1948—the year that van Wijnendaele's sentence for collaboration was lifted—the organizers of Europe's biggest races realized more change was needed. They needed to make the sport more international—*mondialisation* as later generations called it—or have it settle into parochialism. The organizers were all newspaper publishers and they had a vested interest. They could make their own races bigger and more exciting and they could keep the interest going and stoke up international rivalries and do a lot of good for their sales.

Each nation's newspaper would thereby increase interest in races run by the others.

The sports pages had until then written of a small and eventually monotonous band of domestic riders competing against each other. There were national teams in the Tour de France and the world championship, and now and then foreign riders added color to one-day races. But to make the race international, to make every big race a championship, to pitch one country's knights against another's, that would sell newspapers before and long after the race. And in 1948 there was still no competition from television, and international radio broadcasts were scratchy and uncertain.

The Challenge Desgrange-Colombo was also in the spirit of post-war reconciliation. It was impossible to forget what had happened during the war but now it was time to move on, however difficult that might be. And if grudges still remained between nations, well that would simply add spice. Far better to see revenge exacted in a bike race than to go back to war.

The Challenge was the predecessor of all the season-long competitions that followed. Named after the editors of *L'Équipe* in France and *La Gazetta dello Sport* in Italy, it also embraced *Het Nieuwsblad-Sportwereld* and *Les Sports* in Belgium. Riders were to be classed by their placings in the Tours of France and Italy, Milan–San Remo, Paris–Roubaix, the Ronde, the Flèche Wallonne, Paris–Brussels, Paris–Tours and the Tour of Lombardy. Other races were added later. Briek Schotte was the first winner; another Belgian, Fred De Bruyne, won in each of the competition's last three years, from 1956 to 1958.

The first Ronde (with a staggering 265 participants) with Challenge points was won by Schotte, his second victory but this time against foreign competition. Not that the foreigners made much impression, because the first five—in a sprint started by Schotte himself—were Belgian. Not until sixth place, with Cor Bakker of Holland, was there a foreigner. Bakker was more a track rider. His natural terrain was the indoor track, where he rode 18 six-days and won one, in Barcelona in 1952. He even started the Tour de France in 1948; riding the Ronde with the fitness of a winter of six-days seems to have been his preparation for the Tour. He got as far as the sixth stage, where a crash put him outside the time limit and sent him home to Zaandam a week after he had left it.

In 1948, by the way, there were 100 francs "for the last rider to reach Eeklo", one of the many primes—often in kind—that were a feature of the race. Other years had prizes for the first soldier, and 10 kilograms of coffee for the first three Frenchmen, and only Frenchmen, to pass the coffee company that offered it.

"Foreigners had the greatest trouble dealing with our Flandrians," van Wijnendaele wrote of 1948. The Dutch and Italians had been in early offensives but they'd faded when the race hit the worst cobbles. But his gloating stuck in his throat. Foreigners were about to show it was domestic riders who weren't equal to the best and not the other way round. And one foreigner in particular. In 1949.

For years, Fiorenzo Magni had been the Third Man of Italian cycling. Overshadowed first by Gino Bartali and then by his younger upstart, Fausto Coppi, Magni had further problems. He had been too close to the fascists for comfort, given the way the war turned out.

But there's no doubting his courage. Raphaël Géminiani, a contemporary, said: "Magni did nothing gracefully. His successes were hacked out with an ax. His tactics, always the same, were to use force. He wore out rivals by his attacks and his strength. He should have achieved more but the Bartali-Coppi rivalry created an obstacle. And he was never a climber, although there was nobody better at descending. Magni was always Magni."

The man himself said: "I had never been to Belgium. But I had heard and read in the newspapers that the roads were rough. So I thought it would be a good idea to use wooden rims, which are less rigid than traditional ones. It was hard to find those rims but I found out that Clément produced them. Then I had a special kind of tubulars made, larger and heavier than the normal ones. And I put foam rubber all round the handlebars. I remember cold, terrible weather. I was in my element! Thanks to Mother Nature, cold, windy, rainy or snowy days were music to my ears. It was the same with extreme heat."

He traveled to Belgium by train. The race was opened by another star attracted by the new Challenge—Ferdy Kübler, a lean, beak-nosed Swiss who was anything but his national stereotype of respectable caution. While half the stories surrounding him are untrue, he says—he accuses Raphaël Géminiani of inventing most of them—there was no doubting his eccentricity or his wild talent.

Kübler attacked with Louis Thiétard, a strong-jawed Frenchman who won little better than a race a year—23 wins in 19 years—but who had clung to van Steenbergen for as long as he could in 1946. His sec-

Fiorenzo Magni (far right, winning the race): ugly as a pug and so much better than the home guys.

ond place that year was a fluke and nobody took any notice. But they did care about Kübler. And so the race came back together at the feeding station at Izegem. It was there that Louis Caput profited from the lull and attacked. He was to be taken seriously. The journalist René de Latour said of him in *Sporting Cyclist*: "Everybody liked Louis Caput, who became known to the crowds as P'tit Louis. And not only was Caput a likable rider, he was a clever one who knew his job perfectly and I don't think I have ever seen him make a mistake on the road."

Caput was what the French call a *client*: a customer. He won stages of the Tour and in 1946 he was national champion. There wasn't much chance he'd succeed there in Belgium but he was a good guy to have by your side, so the others jumped to be there. Among them: Schotte, Raymond Impanis and Nest Sterckx. Some joined and others left. But by the end there were 18 and the best was Magni, by a length.

A quarter of a century had passed since a foreigner won the Ronde and now here was Magni wounding Belgium and rubbing salt into those wounds. Because next year he won by more than two minutes. And how the others suffered…

"Oh how I remember 1950," Schotte said. "Thanks to the weather, it was a dreadful Ronde. Snow, hail and wind that bit into your fingers and into your face. I was with Magni, Mahé and van Est when I punctured. It was so cold that I could scarcely replace the tire. And then I couldn't get my wheel back in because of my frozen fingers. I had butterfly nuts on the hubs and a spectator had to do them up. I must have lost five minutes. And I set off on the chase of my life. I caught the others and left them. Caput managed to stay with me but in the end I rode away from him as well. Magni could never have won without my bad luck, I'm convinced of that. He had five minutes' lead on me on the Wall of Grammont, but by the finish he only had two left."

Magni smirked at the "only." In 1951 he won by five and a half minutes, after a lone ride of 75 kilometers. He won enough intermediate prizes to buy a house. Prizes had risen along with the status of the race. "At least they left us our eyes to weep," van Wijnendaele lamented, his pride in Belgium reduced to a limp.

Magni—*Il leone delle Fiandre*—opened a business selling motorbikes in 1951 and then trained only in his spare time. He had seen the future: bike factories which had sponsored professional teams—the only businesses *allowed* to sponsor teams—no longer had the sales and therefore the money. He wasn't the first to break cycling's rules and go outside the trade—the first was probably the ITP soccer betting company in Britain in 1947—but his was the most serious breach. No longer sure of backing from Atala, Bianchi, Legnano or other Italian bike firms, he turned to Nivea, a German cosmetics company. Riders had used Nivea to soften the leather inserts of their shorts, lessening the risk of sores. The cream was made, though, as a skin preparation, a beauty aid for women. And other riders, who disliked his fascist sympathies, were quick to point out that the balding, heavy-browed Magni needed more beauty treatment than most.

Nivea gave him 20 million lire, about $260,000. No more than loose change remained by the end of the year, but Nivea, Magni said, made a good profit. "If you remember that cycling was more popular than soccer, and that I was the first to do this, then you can understand the success of this action. Nivea always thanked me for my idea, even years later."

By 1956 business took more time than racing and so he stopped. He ran a car dealership in Monza, northeast of Milan. He died in 2012 when he was 91, shadowed even in death by the fact that he joined Mussolini's fascist party in 1943 and by accusations that he helped round up partisans at Valibona in the Appenines. He denied it and, as ever, there is coincidence and even contradiction in the tale. The romance is that a victim of the round-up, lying in the light of a burning house, looked up to see his cycling hero standing over him. The British writer, William Fotheringham, said: "As was often the case in those turbulent years of mixed and divided loyalties, the picture is not as simple as it seems. Other documents indicate that Magni fought with partisans near the northern town of Monza in 1945."

To forgive or to condemn? It's no longer clear. What *is* clear is that Magni was looking at 30 years in jail and may have gone there had another rider, Alfredo Martini, not spoken in his favor. He was released.

That such a man should dominate the Ronde after a war in which the Germans had encouraged the race to continue, in which Italy had fought on both sides, and in a half of Belgium (the north) that the other half (the south) accused of being too close to their German neighbors, is another layer in a race which all along has been a symbol of Flemish ascendancy.

Just one thing is certain: Magni never needed the bottles of massage oil awarded to the last four in 1949.

They go into a mixture of unconsciousness but at the same time extreme concentration. When they come out of the classics, the riders are psychologically empty.

—Thierry Bricaud, team manager

5
Modern Times And Major Tom

In 1951 the Ronde took another step into the modern era. It allowed limited help from team cars and formalized what had long been happening, letting riders combine with others from the same team: the gloriously phrased *onderlinge verstandhouding en wederzijdse hulp*. Things always look more exciting in Dutch.

From 1955 competitors could take a bike from a teammate but not from a car. A year later, a mechanic could give a rider a wheel with an inflated tire. And by the end of the decade the rules had become largely what they are now. All along, though, the Ronde had been behind current practice, behind what happened in France and Italy. It eased its rules through international pressure and because sponsors were putting in more money and didn't want their riders eliminated through no fault of their own.

Combining on the road may have been illegal until 1951 but it was scarcely unknown, as Briek Schotte made clear from 1952: "I was with Decock and Petrucci in the deciding break. In those days there was still some understanding between Belgian riders. And as the race went on, kilometer after kilometer, we wanted one of us to win rather than a foreigner, even if this Belgian rode for a rival team. So Decock and I agreed to make sure Petrucci lost. We would sprint in turn, one after the other, until he was exhausted. As chance had it, he didn't react the first time Decock attacked. But I got the same money as the winner that day!"

Schotte, in 1950, was made a *Chévalier de l'Ordre de Léopold II*, the award that Karel van Wijnendaele received two years later. Schotte retired in 1959, managed pro teams for 30 years, and died on the day of

the Ronde van Vlaanderen in 2004. In 1940, at 20, he was the youngest in the race; at almost 40 in 1959, he was the oldest.

Record of Briek Schotte, Lion of Flanders

1940	3rd
1941	abandoned after three flats
1942	winner
1943	18th after problems with 6 kilometers to go
1944	2nd
1945	21st
1946	3rd
1947	abandoned after two flats
1948	winner
1949	3rd
1950	2nd
1951	abandoned, ill
1952	3rd
1953	15th
1954	21st
1955	24th
1956	8th
1957	21st
1958	6th
1959	abandoned, broken saddle

Belgium took a long time to recover its pride. The stumpy, barrel-chested Wim van Est—a great raconteur and first Dutchman to wear the *maillot jaune*, in which he plunged over the side of the col d'Aubisque next day and had to be pulled out by rope and tires—won in 1953, Louison Bobet won in 1955 and another Frenchman, Jean Forestier, in 1956. That was the last French win until Jacky Durand in 1992.

Only then could order return, with Fred De Bruyne in 1957, riding for an Italian sponsor, then other Belgians every year until 1964. With one exception. But we'll get to him in a moment. Right now, let's pause in 1953, alongside Wim van Est.

There has never been, surely in any sport, as wonderful a story-teller as the man whose nicknames included Ijzeren Willem—Iron Will: in

English, the joke works both ways. He lived in a quite ordinary house in St Willebrord, a village just large enough to call itself a town, in southern Holland close to the Belgian border. Such is the passion for cycling there that villagers held raffles to raise the money to have a stage of the Tour finish there in 1978. The field included a member of the village club, Aad van de Hoek. His was the 46th Tour appearance by a Willebrord rider.

Club members have worn the Tour yellow jersey for 20 days. The first, and the first Dutchman generally, was van Est in 1951. That was the summer he skidded on the col d'Aubisque in the Pyrenees, fell over the edge and had to be pulled out of the ravine with the team car's tow rope knotted to 40 racing tires. The tires stretched so much as they pulled him up that they no longer fitted their wheels and the Holland team had to go home.

An evening spent with van Est was to listen to a monologue of tales that would have earned him a fortune as an after-dinner speaker had his Dutch not been close to incomprehensible because of his accent and dialect. He could tell, with tears of amusement, how he had been caught rustling a cow by night from Belgium into Holland during world war two, of how he had insisted in court that all he had wanted was the rope and that at dawn he was astonished to find a cow on the other end. He loved to tell of how he and his teenage friends couldn't afford anything but water when they were training, a shortage they got round by staging crashes outside convenient shops and waiting until a shocked shopkeeper came out with something sweet to help with the shock.

He never laughed so much about the Ronde in 1953. Why? Because his team manager, Lomme Driessens, was "the biggest gangster I have ever met" and, according to van Est, repeatedly contrived to prevent his winning so that a more favored rider could succeed instead. Driessens' name will return repeatedly during the Ronde story and rarely in a flattering light.

That day, April 5, the Ronde followed what had become a traditional route from Gent to Eeklo, then to Brugge before going a little further west to turn down toward the French border at Kortrijk to ride through Oudenaarde, over the Wall at Geraardsbergen before reaching the finish at Wetteren. The day was just as cold, wet and windy as a Ronde day is supposed to be.

The weather and the lack of spring fitness were too much for Louison Bobet, who attacked on the Edelare and caused a lot of hearts to flurry but whose initiative then died out. The others saw him tiring

Wim van Est, 1953: "Take a bribe? No, we'll fight to the end!"

and attacked before he could recover. Van Est was among the leaders, along with one of his teammates, Désiré Keteleer.

Like Driessens, Keteleer lived in the Brussels suburb of Vilvoorde, where decades later Sean Kelly also lived. Driessens rated Keteleer as a great hope, even though he was stronger in multi-day races than in classics. He wanted Keteleer to win; above all, he didn't want a Dutchman, van Est, to win.

Driessens drove up beside the break of four. "Ask van Est what he'll take to give you the victory," he shouted at Keteleer. Van Est overheard. Reporters say he replied "Take? We're fighting this out to the end." But the language was a great deal stronger. The idea that Driessens, van Est and Keteleer could all be in the same team, that the team constituted half the break, and that nevertheless money was expected to change hands between teammates didn't strike Driessens as strange.

Driessens, van Est says, never wanted him to win and would do anything to stop him. Once, he insisted—and just when and where it happened is hazy—Driessens paid a signalman to close railroad crossing gates in front of him. Van Est, who had been in trouble before for leaping over gates, waited angrily for a train that never came.

Van Est won the Ronde by 2 seconds, beating Keteleer, with Bernard Gauthier third at 45 seconds and Bobet at 1 minute 40 seconds. The club at Willebrord treated him as a hero, of course. And the Garin bike company that employed him paid him the bonus it had promised. Van Est invested it back into the company along with much of his savings, reckoning that 135,000 guilders in shares would pay twice as much as the bank interest he could get in Holland.

By then, though, Garin was struggling. It couldn't hold its place in a bike market that was already being eaten away by a fad for small motorbikes. The factory's managers reacted too late and the business failed—taking van Est's savings with it.

Which brings us to that exception in 1961 Ronde. That was the year the race went to an Englishman, a professional for only two years beating the Italian champion, Nino Defilippis, who had been a pro racer for a decade. Defilippis' record included the Tour of Lombardy and seven stages of the Tour de France. Tom Simpson's record was 29th in the Tour de France in 1960 and a win in the Tour du Sud-Est which pleased him and the few back in Britain who heard about it but really didn't count for anything.

Tom Simpson was a local for the Ronde because he lived in Mariakerke, a suburb of Gent. The papers loved him because he delighted in pulling faces for photographers, grinning, grimacing, sometimes poking out his tongue. His face—and the advertising on his jersey—would then get in the papers. He'd ridden his last race in Britain in 1959 and then moved to western France to make it as a bike rider and to avoid compulsory service in the army. Then he'd moved to Belgium to be closer to the everyday village races that made much of his income. That day in 1961, he stuck his tongue out at his Italian rival. He sprinted, never his strength, then buckled his legs a little and grimaced to suggest he had made his effort too early. Defilippis knew that was the moment to sprint harder. He did. And it didn't work out.

Simpson remembered: "I started my sprint about a kilometer from the line, and as I anticipated, Defilippis took my wheel. With 300 meters to go, I feigned that I had blown up and slowed slightly. Immediately the Italian took a flyer off my wheel and passed me on the right, going like a train for the line.

"As he went, I restarted sprinting, really going flat out, and drew almost alongside him on his right. I reasoned that he would look back to see where I was, and since he had gone by me on the right, he would look to his left. He did just that and got the shock of his life for I was nowhere in sight. In the split second it took him to turn his head to opposite side, I went past him. He had slowed momentarily through being taken by surprise like that, and I was over the line just a wheel in front of him.

Cycling reported: "Italian pride had taken a severe knock. Defilippis lodged a protest, claiming he hadn't seen the finish line because the banner had been blown away by high winds. Simpson retorted that Defilippis had crossed the line three times on the finishing circuit and had plenty of opportunity to get his bearings. The Italians tried another tack—the line was not clearly marked out and was difficult to see.

"Finally the Italians asked Simpson to agree to an equal first decision. 'They told me that an Italian had not won a classic since 1953,' said Simpson. 'But I replied that an Englishman had not won one since 1896! I was not going to be talked out of anything.'"

Simpson's talent for publicity put him in a sharp suit and bowler hat to play Major Thompson. The major, unknown outside France, was the satirical creation of a French author who had worked with British troops and their officers during the war and noted their mannerisms and the amused way they treated the French as foreigners in their own country. The *Notebooks of Major Thompson*—the author didn't own up for a while—delighted French readers with its leg-pulling observations of their foibles.

The idea that there could actually *be* someone British called Thompson, a combination of Simpson's first and last names, appealed to his agent, Daniel Dousset. Simpson was to dress as an expatriate major and be pictured drinking tea while reading *The Times*. Simpson, a miner's son who'd done all he could to avoid real majors, played the role with dry amusement.

Keeping Simpson in the public eye struck Dousset as important. His *poulain* injured his knee after winning the Ronde and missed much of the rest of that season. He had a retainer from his sponsor, the St-Raphaël apéritif company, but he won just £500 all year with more from his few races that paid appearance money. It was "barely enough to live on," he wrote—which shows that winning even Belgium's biggest race guaranteed nothing. Simpson's appearance money had tumbled to £80, a fifth of what he'd expect. Dousset, not for the last time, needed to keep him in the public eye, to keep him earning the money from which he'd take his percentage.

That need for money proved his undoing. Simpson won the world championship in 1965 by improbably outsprinting the hefty German, Rudi Altig. That should have guaranteed him his biggest pay packet of a lifetime, thanks to track and criterium appearances. But Simpson went skiing that winter and broke a leg. The 1966 summer that should have paid so well was a disappointment. On top of that, his place in the Peugeot team was threatened by a rising Eddy Merckx. The rules then limited the number of foreign riders in a team and Simpson looked like losing not only his leadership of a French team but even his place in that team.

The 1967 Tour was where Simpson had to impress other sponsors, to get into another team. It was disputed by national teams. Simpson would have weaker riders alongside him in British colours—white with a Union Jack on each shoulder—but they would have a loyalty he couldn't be sure of with Peugeot. Dousset told him the broken leg and a run of poor performances had brought his contract value to nothing. Simpson needed a good Tour to put himself back in the market. Otherwise the end of his career was looming.

"He left Gent that year with winning the Tour as his ambition," said his wife, Helen.

Simpson picked Mont Ventoux as his set piece. He fell and died just short of the summit, drugged and dehydrated.

The 1964 race that finally ended the Belgian run that Simpson had interrupted went to Rudi Altig, the German who had come second to Simpson in the world championship at San Sebastian. Altig, who still rides a bike regularly, delighted track audiences as an amateur by standing on his head between races. It was a yoga routine at which he excelled. Others teased him about it, even in his professional years, but Altig had the last laugh. He once left a restaurant at La Rochelle by walking on his hands; other riders with him, including Simpson, tried to copy him but collapsed. While Altig passed through the door upside down, they were reduced to retrieving coins that had fallen from their pockets.

What gave Altig his Ronde win, apart from talent, was one of the civil wars that so often rage in Belgian cycling. The expected winner was Rik van Looy, a short and heavy-thighed sprinter with short shorts

Rik van Looy, denied a world championship by a little cheating – or was he?

and a smile like a Halloween melon. He held a grip over Belgian cycling and whatever else he could grasp, thanks to his say in who would ride in his teams and who would get to ride, or more important *not* ride, the village races that gave lesser riders most of their earnings.

"The tactic in van Looy's team," said Englishman Vin Denson, who rode with him in the scarlet jersey of Solo, "was that van Looy should win." Beyond that, nothing was planned. When it didn't happen or van Looy chose not to race seriously, the not-too-bright and uncouth youths whom van Looy often employed as domestiques scrapped as much between themselves as with those they were supposed to defeat.

Jan Janssen, the Dutch former world champion and Tour winner who now lives a handful of meters inside Belgium in the village of Putte, said of van Looy: "As a rider, none better. As a man, *niks*." He pulled a face as he said it. Not for nothing was van Looy referred to as the *keizer*, the emperor.

"The Ronde was a race that suited me," van Looy said. "If I was up there, I could always win the sprint. Unfortunately I so often had trouble that I wasn't there at the finish." Broken bikes cost him the race in 1954 and 1955 and, in 1957, a flat tire as he came down the Wall of Geraardsbergen just as Fred De Bruyne attacked and went on to win. Things were even worse in 1958, when he flatted and, having got going again, snapped his frame shortly afterward. There were just 20 kilometers to the finish and the rules didn't yet allow riders to take a complete new bike from a following car. He did get permission to take a teammate's bike instead but the time that the exchange took was the margin by which he lost the race.

And so to the Ronde of 1964, and some more background. Several things made the race interesting. There were more cobbled climbs than usual, for a start. And the 40 riders clear at the foot of the Edelare included van Looy and a lesser Belgian, Benoni Beheyt. Lesser, that is, except that Beheyt wore the rainbow stripes of world champion. Which wasn't to van Looy's liking.

The previous year's world championship had been in Ronse, in West Flanders. Van Looy came from the other side of Flanders, from Herentals, but this was his home crowd nevertheless and he expected to win. Even to be allowed to win, at least by fellow Belgians. Among those was Beheyt, just 23, so unconsidered that nobody waited for him when he punctured on the penultimate lap. He got back to the race just in time to hear the bell.

Van Looy was much exercised by an attack by his supposed team-mate, Gilbert Desmet, who was showing unusual form. Desmet had responded to a move from Simpson and collected a small but workable lead. That angered van Looy because, in Simpson's words: "The Belgians blocked everything because van Looy was again offering his teammates good money if they helped him to victory. 50,000 Belgian francs or £350 per man was the price he offered and, one way or another, they managed to ruin the whole race…"

Beheyt remembered: "Desmet was on the way to denying van Looy the third world championship that he wanted. He would have been better to leave the chase to the foreigners. He panicked and went to the front too soon. He asked me to lead out the sprint for him. I said I had cramp so that I could get out of it. I wanted to get on his wheel, not to beat him but to be able to stand on the podium with him.

"Well, Rik was really on an off-day and he wasn't thinking properly. He was so anxious that he started the sprint himself, hit the wind too soon and began fading at 300 meters."

Van Looy, realizing what had happened, rode to the edge of the road, alongside the barrier, for more shelter. Beheyt drew up alongside as the others attacked and what happened next depends on whose story you hear. Beheyt says he fended off van Looy so that he didn't fall off himself. Others say he grabbed van Looy's jersey and tugged. What everybody says is that van Looy never forgave him.

The truth is mixed. Cycling is business as much as sport and van Looy and Beheyt profited from increased fees at "revenge" races all round Europe. But the two never rode in the same team and, when it mattered, van Looy was happy when Beheyt lost. That day in 1964, Rudi Altig broke away just before the Valkenberg and van Looy did nothing to chase. That deterred the others, who saw no reason to rush after a world-class pursuiter and take with them a world-class sprinter who was sure to beat them. As for van Looy, he had been the first Flandrian to win both the Ronde and Paris–Roubaix in a world champion's jersey, in 1962, and he wasn't going to let Beheyt copy him. Each watched the other and Altig won by 4 minutes 5 seconds after riding alone for 60 kilometers including into the wind of the North Sea.

The bunch was right to expect to be beaten but it forecast the wrong man. Beheyt beat them instead and van Looy languished in tenth place. Not the mechanical trouble that had stopped his winning other races—just a clash with the wrong man on the wrong day.

An interesting observation from Graham Webb, the world amateur road champion in 1967: "Van Looy always did try to be and look posh, but you could see through the act of this working class lad. I think he was trying to emulate Coppi, who was very fanatical about looking the gentleman. The done thing in those days: look at Tom [Simpson] in his bowler. I've raced with van Looy and he always had a neatly folded handkerchief, to blow his nose on, in his racing shorts pocket. Whereas all the other riders would just blow their snot out all over the peloton! He felt too big for that."

Karel Van Wijnendaele died in 1961. He had managed a trade team— Cycles Marcel Buysse—then coached the national team and from 1930 to 1948 he picked and managed the country's teams for the Tour de France. He wrote more than 11,000 articles. He was a race commissaire, a track director, and general secretary of the Belgian federation. He had managed riders and taken them to six-days as far away as the USA. He had a stable of horses at his villa in St-Martens-Latem, the first bought in the USA in 1935. Trotting was the only sport he wrote about outside cycling. From 1935 to 1939 he had what was described as the largest trotting stable in Europe. The war, and declining health, ended all that but he kept his favorite horses, called Iron and Happiness.

Towards the end of his life he became forgetful and lost track of the era. Nora, his granddaughter, was too young to know him well. But she remembered he always gave her 100 francs on new year's day. "That was a lot of money in his time but by the end of the Fifties it was almost nothing. But he stuck to his traditions," she said. He could also be hazy about tax. He bought land and houses but forgot, according to his son, Willem, that "on every house you sold, you had to pay 25 per cent in tax, so for every four houses you sold, you lost one."

Van Wijnendaele died at Deinze on December 20 and he's remembered by a monument on the Ronde route at the summit of the Kwaremont. It's there through the collaboration of Willem and a rich landowner, the Baron Behaeghel. The landowner was French—his family had moved to Belgium with the rise of Napoleon—and the title of baron had vanished centuries earlier. But traditions held and that was how he was known.

The two men met in the Chez Georgette, a bar at the top of the Oude Kwaremont. There they drank a beer and agreed that a monument could be erected on land on the southern ascent of the hill, which happened to mark the border between Dutch-speaking Flanders and French-speaking Wallonia. The agreement was written on the back of a beermat and signed.

Van Wijnendaele is remembered too by a cyclo-sportive, and by a club named after him at St-Martens-Latem, where he lies in the churchyard. He moved to the village from Gent in 1939, calling his house *Hof van Sportwereld* or sometimes *Huize Sportwereld*. He is also honored by a plaque outside the house in the Burgplaats in Torhout where he lived with his first wife: "Here lived Karel van Wijnendaele, the pioneer of Flemish cycling."

Willem adopted his father's pen name and covered several Tours de France as a journalist. Willem's daughter, Nora, reverted to Steyaert and joined the fledgling national television service in 1953 to present children's shows. Ten years later she had her own show, *Eenmaal per jaar* (Once a year).

Willem van Wijnendaele, a square-headed man remarkably similar to his father, with white hair, glasses and uneven teeth bared in a ready smile, died in 1973.

Karel van Wijnendaele's death brought a new way of thinking. The essence of the Ronde van Vlaanderen, people began to realize, was akin to Paris–Roubaix on other side of the border. Paris–Roubaix had its cobbles but the Ronde had both cobbles and hills. Now alarms were ringing. The ragged roads with body-blackening cinder bike paths were going. Paris–Roubaix risked becoming just another race, a Paris–Tours, a sprinters' race for the North. Peter Post won at better than 45 kilometers per hour in 1964. That was ridiculous. And now the grit, the struggle, of the Ronde van Vlaanderen was also going, drowned in asphalt.

Paris–Roubaix had to go out and find bad roads. Not the roads, the obvious routes, that riders once took but diversions into improbability that would keep alive the race that was "cycling's last great madness," as Jacques Goddet put it.

In Belgium, the only roads the asphalt gangs were likely to leave alone were on the *koppen* and *bergen*. Nothing used those except tractors. And the Ronde. And the Ronde would find those hills and revel in them.

The Ronde's own history says: "After the death of Karel van Wijnendaele, it was urgent that the Ronde find new paths to tread. The spread of asphalt on our Flemish roads demanded that the route planners find new obstacles. They went looking for smaller, cobbled roads and hills, especially in the Schelde valley and the Flemish Ardennes." Until then, the race had avoided rather than sought these roads.

And the Ronde passed through the center of towns and even cities. Riding in a bunch, on cobbles, repeatedly crossing tram lines at a shallow angle, perhaps in the rain, brought a danger that does not exist today. The new organizers couldn't, wouldn't want to, re-create that danger. Not there, anyway. Instead, they could shrug sadly at the general improvement to roads and then send their race up byways that nobody but farmers knew existed. It was then that the Ronde became what is now.

The climbs are short but hard. Some, like the Kluisberg, have been asphalted. But even then it is nearly 1,100 meters long and at times 12 degrees. It spells the end for the weak. And the course winds and turns back on itself to take in hill after hill, sometimes the same hill several times.

The name Oude Kwaremont is a distortion of *kwade remonte*, a dialect combination of Dutch and French meaning… "hard climb." The approach is a race within a race, according to Peter van Petegem. "It's nervous and elbows and shoulders are the order of the day to secure the best spot at the front. You really need to be a nasty bastard and keep your position, but I had no problem with that: I had guts!"

The start is asphalted. Then come 1,600 meters of cobbles, steep at first, then flat, then uphill again.

"It's very important to be in the first two rows," says van Petegem, "in order to get in the right position. What's more, it's important because from this moment on, hills feature regularly in the race. Straight after the Oude Kwaremont there's the steep Paterberg, the even steeper Koppenberg, the Steenbeekdries, the Taaienberg. There's hardly time to catch your breath. If you have to chase from the foot of the Oude Kwaremont, you've lost already."

The Paterberg comes soon afterwards. The race climbs it three times, a novelty hill where until 1986 there'd been nothing. A farmer jealous of a friend who lived close to the Koppenberg retaliated at great expense by spending a year and a half building his own cobbled road across fields in front of his home. He can now watch riders pass at his if not their leisure. And, better still, he can watch them pass in agony because no sooner had he planned the road than the local council at Kluisbergen decided it should be cobbled.

The Paterberg is 375 meters long and 12.5 per cent of narrow cobbled road. Johan Museeuw's assessment was little different from van Petegem's: "The race goes flat out from the Oude Kwaremont to the Paterberg. From the foot of one to the top of the other, there's not a single moment when the pressure eases. It's flat out."

The bunch drops off the N36 main road and down into what passes locally for a valley. The course then takes them to the left and up the Paterberg. "The bunch takes these tiny roads at 60 kilometers per hour. An ordinary rider would lose three minutes in just these three kilometers compared to a pro. The golden rule, which applies right the way round the Ronde, is never to touch the brakes. Decelerate and you instantly lose 10 to 20 places."

The race turns right on to the Paterberg, which rises like a wall. "You have to go into it at full speed. The bend is tight but I promise you you never touch the brakes. The steepness is like the Koppenberg, although the Koppenberg's cobbles are worse."

The last 100 meters are the hardest, not just because they're the top of the hill but because it takes an out-of-the-saddle effort to maintain speed.

"You have to be able to explode in the second part of the climb," Museeuw says. "The third time you go up it is the toughest, and if the road is wet and the cobbles slippery, even the stars have a difficult time."

Gabé Konrad caught the spirit of the Koppenberg: "So narrow is the Kopp that spectators have to pile themselves on the steep banks that line the hill, waiting for the inevitable *valpartijen*, pile-ups, on the slippery stones. For years, competitors would come to a grinding halt when they hit the steep embankment, clenching teeth and slipping to the lowest gears. Inevitably a crawling racer would fall, sending followers toppling like dominoes, hoisting their rigs to their shoulders and running, cyclo-cross style, sliding around on their cleats. *Valpartij!*

Fans flocked to the Kopp to ooh and aah and laugh, but the riders were disgusted and, at times, humiliated."

Bernard Hinault, who rode the race only once, had a row with the organizers and then stayed away in disgust, wrote in his autobiography: "It's hard to explain what the Koppenberg means to a racing cyclist. It's a cobbled wall, a kilometer long, not properly surfaced and so steep that the race cars sometimes get stuck on it. It's narrow and completely enclosed. There are spectators above it and publicity posters everywhere. Only the first five or six riders have any chance: the rest fall off or scramble up as best they can. I swore not to ride the Ronde again."

The danger of the Ronde's narrow and badly surfaced hills came close to tragedy in 1987. A Danish rider, Jesper Skibby, had ridden ahead of the race with a Belgian, Ludo Schurgers. He was exhausted when he reached the Koppenberg. It was his second season as a professional, he was riding his first Ronde and he was close to losing two minutes' lead. He was struggling on the climb, riding in the right gutter which was slightly smoother than the cobbles, when a grey BMW approached from behind. Race car number 7 had the registration C3733 beneath its radiator grill and an identifying panel attached to the front bumper beneath the left-side headlights. It held the international commissaire. A gray-haired official in a gray sleeveless jacket stood with his head through the sun roof. The car's driver was anxious to pass Skibby before the rest of the swarmed up behind. He tried to overtake.

At that moment Skibby struggled even more and turned a meter to the left at 45 degrees. The car hit his back wheel and Skibby fell to the right, strapped into his pedals, sitting on the lowest part of a grass bank. The driver stopped and for a moment the car moved backwards. Then it moved forward again, pushing a spectator into the steep grass bank on the left and driving over Skibby's back wheel on the right. The official with his head through the roof looked back over his shoulder as another spectator began to chase him up the hill, waving his arms. The crowd began to jeer and boo. But the driver kept going to the finish, afraid to stop because the race wasn't far behind.

As though that weren't enough, a yellow car with *Het Nieuwsblad* painted on the side brushed against a man who'd gone to help Skibby.

The race commissaire continued to the finish, where the crowd—which had seen everything on giant screens showing the repeated slow-motions broadcast by Belgian television—threw stones, cups, bottles and anything else they could find. It overshadowed a first win by a French-speaking Belgian, Claude Criquielion.

The episode gave Skibby "a strange but undeniable popularity," remembered the French journalist, Florian Joyard. He got more publicity for himself and his sponsor than if he had won the race, said a former rider, Roger Swerts. But while Skibby won a stage of the Tour de France, three of the Tour of Spain, and one of the Giro, he started using steroids in 1991, human growth hormone and testesterone in 1992, and EPO in 1993, treated by a doctor in exchange for 7.5 per cent of his winnings. Facts he admitted in his autobiography.

Skibby retired with an injured knee in 2000 and worked in public relations for the Home-Jack and Jones team, then for a youth team, finally dropping out of the sport in 2002. He has epileptic seizures caused by banging his head in a crash in Tirreno–Adriatico in 1993.

The Koppenberg didn't return until the surface had been improved in 2002. And then, cars were banned. But the absence didn't please everybody. Roger De Vlaeminck, for instance, said: "That should never have disappeared from the course. It's like taking the cobbles away from Paris–Roubaix." But the hill went, then returned and in 2003 the road was again improved, at a cost of €638,000 paid by the regional administration. But in 2007 the climb vanished again, after only a dozen riders rode to the top the previous year, the rest forced to walk or run because of crashes in front of them.

Wim van Herreweghe, the head of the race, said: "We want to avoid having the smooth running of the race too disturbed by non-sporting elements, above all if it's raining and given the current state of the cobbles." It made De Vlaeminck cross. Complaints that it falsified the result were themselves false, he said: Hennie Kuiper had won the Ronde in 1981 even though he was last over the Koppenberg.

In 1993 the roads minister in Flanders, Johan Sauwens, answered a prayer that van Wijnendaele had made back in 1963: "Father, if I may ask you something, make sure, please, that the Kwaremont is never covered with tar and that for as long as there is a Ronde this East Flanders road will stay in its recent state. With, next to the bad stone road, a bike path a meter and a half wide where riders have to go and where they can barely get by. Let the Ronde, this one road race in the world, remain the Ronde."

Sauwens answered his plea in 1993 by preserving close on 34 kilometers of cobbles as a national monument. The man in charge of maintenance and restoration, Armand Bruyland, chief engineer of roads at Oudenaarde, explained: "After the site was abandoned for 15 years, it was classified by the Flemish ministry of culture, so it has the same status as the cathedral in Brugge. So we had to use all the original stones, and only those stones, and take them all up the length of the road and then replace them. The road had to be relaid so that the Ronde could ride it. It had become impracticable because the clay soil made it very unstable."

His solution was to put drainage beneath the road, then lay a bed of cement, sand and cinders, and cover the whole lot with clean gravel so that rain would flow through.

That's not to say that *all* cobbles either in Flanders or even relevant to the Ronde have been saved. Even the Kwaremont wasn't safe: 400 meters were asphalted two years after van Wijnendaele appealed to heaven. The rest was done the following year.

Roads that head straight up hills rather than around them are the safest. They see the least conventional traffic and therefore hinder other road-users least. They are recognized for their tourist appeal.

"People often refer to the cobbles as Napoleonic," Bruyland said, "but they're not. They're rounded, the sort that we call baby's heads— *kinderkopjes*—in Dutch. The Koppenberg is the 'hill of heads': the cobbles are rounder here than elsewhere."

It's had that name for a long time. A map in 1770 shows the western side of the hill as the Coppenbergh and the eastern side as the Rotelenbergh. The spelling has changed since to Rotelenberg and it's that side, along a road named the Steengat (stone hole), that the Ronde usually rides. The other side, now cemented, is both shallower and smoother.

Close to the bottom is a bar with pictures of Freddy Maertens in a red and white Flandria jersey, the one that had a different main sponsor every year, another of Roger De Vlaeminck in the season in which money persuaded him to ride beside Francesco Moser in a Sanson team troubled by their subsequent rivalry, and Jean-Luc Vandenbroucke, uncle of the more talented but more tormented Frank Vandenbroucke, in a white Peugeot jersey with a black checkered band designed to look distinctive on monochrome television.

Missing from the display is the rider who persuaded the organizers to use the hill. Harry van den Bremt, a journalist at *Het Nieuwsblad* who was the race organizer, said: "At the start of the '70s, I got a call from Walter Godefroot, who told me 'I've just been over something in

Walter Godefroot, 1978: "Hey, look, there's this hill I've just found..."

Flanders where you've never been. It wouldn't be bad for the Ronde...'" Godefroot couldn't, however, say just where the hill was. Or, according to the story that he tells himself, he said he wouldn't say where the hill was until he'd retired—otherwise he'd have to race up it.

The Koppenberg is just a narrow road from and to nowhere in particular, other than a junction with a secondary highway, and nothing was done. Then a few years later van den Bremt called him back and said: "Listen, you told me a while back that you knew somewhere…" And he went out to find it.

History, as ever, has two versions. Godefroot said he spoke not to van den Bremt but to a former pro called Noël Foré, whose job it was to find new and disagreeable roads. In the end, Godefroot said, it was the owner of the house at the top of the hill who gave Foré and van den Bremt the name.

Godefroot said: "They straight away called me, to announce that they'd discovered my secret. I was horrified at the idea of having to go over it in a race."

Walter Godefroot, a shy man with a pudgy face and sometimes staring eyes, won the Ronde in 1968 and 1978. And he won the final Tour de France stage in 1975 when it finished for the first time on the Champs Elysées. He became a team manager with a troubled history, having to deny claims from a soigneur, Jef D'Hondt, that he was "behind the system of organized doping in the [Telekom] team in the middle of the 1990s." A court sided with him and in 2013 ordered D'Hondt—described as "a demi-god in the world of soigneurs" by Festina's Willy Voet—to pay €7,500 in damages. But seven of the team's riders said they had taken drugs while Godefroot was manager, although Godefroot said he may have been naive but he wasn't responsible.

Not that D'Hondt, a silver-haired man with a crumpled face, was strange to this world himself. In 2000 he copped a suspended nine-month jail sentence and a fine of 20,000 francs (about €3,000) for doping offenses on the fringe of the Festina scandal that almost brought an end to the Tour de France in 1998.

Godefroot drove one of the official cars for the Ronde until his 70th birthday. Harry van den Bremt, the jovial, round-faced man who was head of cycling at *Het Nieuwsblad* for 36 years and for 22 years editor of *Vélo*, an annual directory of riders and results, died of cancer in 2004.

As for the Koppenberg, that came into the race in 1976 and stayed until Skibby's wheel-crushing in 1987. It then disappeared for 15 years, at the end of which Armand Bruyland began his renovation. The hill returned in 2002 but deteriorated again. It was kept out of the race in 2007, the Ronde going instead up the Kortekeer again and trying a new hill, the Eikenmolen (oak mills). More repairs were made and the Koppenberg returned in 2008.

That pleased Walter Planckaert, the winner in 1976. For him, the cobbles of the Koppenberg are as crucial to the race as the cobbles of Paris–Roubaix. "The organizers should never have listened to Bernard Hinault. The Koppenberg is an essential part of the Ronde. The only people to complain are those who can't ride to the top. That sort of hill makes the race hard and it adds to the spectacle which gets people out of their armchair."

He's so committed that he takes youngsters from his club in Aalst over the Koppenberg to convince them they can do it and to teach them the area.

A short time before world war one, a man found guilty of murder was cleared in court in Brussels thanks to the evidence of an old woman who insisted she had seen the man at the moment of the crime, a Sunday morning, in the company of two other people. The police found these two others and they confirmed what the woman had said. "I was on my doorstep when Monsieur X crossed from the other side of the road. It was Sunday, April 30, at 11.05 in the morning."

The judge was astonished.

"But how can you be so certain of that?"

"Because that was the day the Ronde went by and I didn't want to miss that. At 11.05 it had gone by and I could get on with preparing lunch."

The Ronde van Vlaanderen had just saved an innocent man—which is why we can pardon the Ronde for a lot today!

—Memories of Karel van Wijnendaele

6
Ready, Steady, Eddy!

The first year that Eddy Merckx won the Tour de France was the first time a Belgian had won since 1939. Three decades. That year you could buy flags, tea-towels and even balls of chewing gum printed with his face. There was even—until he went to court to suppress it—a poster of his naked backside in a changing room. That incident apart, he had restored Belgian pride beyond the narrow world of cycling and he had done it, what's more, as a linguistic neutral.

Eddy is a French name, short for Edouard. Dutch-speakers form a diminutive by taking the final part of a name: for the Flemish, he would have been Ward. The name Merckx, on the other hand, is not only Dutch but distinctly Belgian. The improbable collection of consonants shows that. So far so good. But, better, he came from Brussels, a largely French-speaking enclave in Dutch-speaking Flanders. He spoke Dutch and French without hesitation. He was the son neither of the rich nor of the toiling folk of factories: his father was a grocer in a bourgeois suburb. His wife, Claudine, has a French name and her mother's decision that the marriage should be celebrated only in French was the one sore point in this divided nation. Especially since the couple's language at home was Dutch.

The problem was that he had never won the Ronde. He had tried and he had failed and men sat in bars and said that he would never do it. The course wasn't made for him, they said. And what's more, his domination of every other race, his first pick of teammates, the prizes he swept up and even how his appearance money reduced the kitty for everyone else, all that led to resentment. Team sponsors, if they were prepared to come into the sport at all, saw better than to spend a lot on riders who would at best come second. They could get more wins and more publicity from a cheaper team that won round-the-houses races.

The outcome was that those not in his team rode as much to defeat him as they did to win. In 1969 Merckx simply got off his bike during the world championship at Zolder, frustrated that every move he made was followed by a dozen men anxious to stop him. So determined were they to stop Merckx that they had no plan for what to do next. A minor Belgian and an unknown criterium rider recruited into the Dutch team at the last moment to make up the numbers escaped and stayed away. Harm Ottenbros, the Dutch stand-in, won. Merckx's tormentors then turned on Ottenbros instead, an unworthy champion. He was never allowed to win anything worth winning. He earned less as world champion than as a criterium rider and within a short time he dropped out of cycling and lived in a squat.

Not that Merckx had made things better for himself. The French historian, Pierre Chany, recalled: "The natural law of sport is that the best should win, and that the best in turn will become the target of others. That was the case with Merckx, who had so often crushed his opponents in 1967. But he had committed 'faults' in the eyes of his opponents. The fault, for example, of ridiculing Italians in the Tour of Sardinia, a second-category race which most riders used for training."

It was an unfortunate side that Merckx had, a lack of discretion and of any understanding that others had to make a living as well, and a reputation for being what the British rider, Barry Hoban, called "the biggest cry-baby in the business" when he didn't win.

That lack of subtlety, and the resistance that it created, led him to ridicule the field in the Ronde of 1969. He would grind the others until they could frustrate him no more. The weather was suitably Wagnerian and Merckx played the Flying Belgian, if not the Flying Dutchman. Rik Vanwalleghem describes 1969 as one of the race's top 10. "While the cream of cycling kept moaning about the awful wind and rain that Flanders had inflicted, the Cannibal [Merckx's nickname, an unflattering allusion to his treatment of others] went off on a cool lone attack for 70 kilometers. His team manager, Driessens, tried to get the great master to ease back a bit and got the less than courteous reply *Kust gij een beetje kloten*' flung at his head."

It's a difficult expression to translate but its color shows a man with a French first name had no trouble with Dutch invective.

Merckx plowed into the wind between Ninove and Nederbrakel, the others on his wheel. And, if it hadn't occurred to him before, he decided he would go no slower if they weren't there and that he might well go faster alone. He attacked repeatedly, shedding more riders each time until, with 70 kilometers to go, he was by himself. It was then that Lomme Driessens drove up in his Peugeot, a mechanic and a federation representative as his passengers, to gesticulate and demand an explanation. And it was then that Merckx told him to, er, mind his own business.

Merckx then minded *his* business. He struggled to get his first 30 seconds' lead but after that the chasers gave up hope. He crossed the Valkenberg with more than two minutes in hand, riding the Kastelstraat with five minutes and finishing five and a half minutes ahead of Felice Gimondi and with eight minutes on the last survivors of an original group of 20.

"It was typical Ronde weather," Merckx remembered years afterwards. "It was cold and raining." As a matter of accuracy, that isn't typical Ronde weather at all; there have been many more days of unremarkable weather than of rain, wind or snow. But bad weather is the reputation and the romance of Ronde day, so…

"Even before the Kwaremont the head of the field was reduced to 22. On the road from Ninove to Nederbrakel we got the wind full in our face. The others began to string out on my wheel. And I thought to myself that if I was going to do all the work on the front, I may just as well ride off alone." And he did, despite Driessens' orders to behave himself and go back to the bunch and await developments.

"At the finish," Merckx said, "Driessens was full of how we had pulled it off together. He was full of that sort of nonsense. We never did get on well. He could make a lot of noise but he knew a lot less about racing and organization."

Curiously, Freddy Maertens has the opposite view. Having adopted Driessens as a father substitute—throughout his life he has been nothing without a dominant figure to tell him what to do—he had his greatest years with him and recalls that his organization was faultless. The extent to which Merckx saw it differently led to his firing Driessens, adding another rival to the cast. Driessens, on the other hand, could point out that it took Merckx six years to win another Ronde without his guidance.

Eric Leman, a Flemish Belgian with a French name, won the Ronde for the third time in 1973. "It comes back to me every day," he said after retiring to work for a company making hygiene products. And to

Eric Leman, 1973: never a day that he doesn't remember.

make sure everyone else remembered it as well, he made sure his business cards listed his victories in 1970, 1972 and 1973. "Until some day someone wins four times, my name will always be linked with the race," he says with a contented smile.

Maybe he needed that little boast on his cards, because he began losing his hair not long after dropping out of racing, and he needed to wear glasses. He soon looked a lot older. Ask about his wins and he'll say: "The first was the best. In 1969 Merckx had made fools of everyone and so 1970 was time for revenge. The weather was rotten. Rain, a vicious headwind, and very cold. Around Torhout, 30 of us got away, including all the favorites. That got whittled down as the race went on until there were just 14. Then eight kilometers before the line, Walter Godefroot went through really hard. I was having a hard time on the cobbles and my legs hurt, but I gave it everything. Because the previous season we had been teammates at Flandria, but Walter didn't want to share the team leadership with me any longer and after some harsh conversations with Pol Claeys, the head of the company, he'd gone off to the Italian Salvarani team. 'You've got to choose,' he told Claeys. 'Having two leaders doesn't work.' And Claeys opted for me. And the rivalry of the previous season kept running through my head.

"With Merckx, we got back to Godefroot on the edge of Merelbeke. I was dying on my bike. And then it got worse. Both of them thought they could win, but alone and without me. So one would attack and then the other, so that I was forced to chase each time. That was terribly painful for my legs but I absolutely refused to be dislodged. It was only my willpower that kept me going.

"Well, I'll remember those last meters, every single one, for a century. Merckx went for a long sprint when we got to the last straight. What surprised me was that he died 300 meters from the line. Was he really dead or had he and Godefroot come to an arrangement to make sure that this new boy, Leman, wouldn't win? Either way, I got to the front too soon. But what should I do? In a fraction of a second I decided to go for it and I left Godefroot by several lengths. Walter came back hard but I held him off. A real sprinter always has a little bit of speed left in those moments."

He was never high on élan. He sprinted, said Gabé Konrad, by "flinging himself frantically at the line, veins bulging, elbows flying. Anybody who was in his way [at the end of races] would have to move or be steamrollered. While some roadmen didn't appreciate his style, especially the plowed-over ones, the Flandrian Belgians loved it." And he matched the Flemish self-image. Where some riders wore two woolen jerseys, he'd wear one but slip an insulating barrier of paper beneath it. He rarely wore gloves and saw overshoes as a hindrance, said the Belgian editor, Noël Truyers. Leman—he says it himself—was the Sean Kelly of his time. A hard man.

He said: "I could look back on a year where I won seven races and ridden a respectable Paris–Nice. But nobody expected I could win a classic as hard as the Ronde van Vlaanderen. Even my teammates at Mars-Flandria couldn't. Roger De Vlaeminck, for instance, who'd been in the leading group with his brother Erik and Jempi Monseré, hadn't taken me seriously."

But life wasn't going to be good for ever. A week before the next Ronde, Leman's wife died in a car crash. Leman won the race twice more, a record, but it was never the same. He retired after nine years as a professional when he was 31.

The Ronde he missed because of his wife was won by Eef Dolman, who as an amateur had won the world championship in 1966 after a hefty dose of amphetamine and a bit of trickery at the drug test. It was a technique he used throughout his career to the point that he was addicted. He was stripped of his Dutch championship in 1967 after cheating the test. The same would have happened in 1965 had he not insisted his doctor had prescribed nose drops.

Dolman was a problem child with a poor school record who took up cycling because his father demanded he find himself a hobby. And, he said himself, he threw himself into it fanatically. But the Ronde, he said, he owed to fortune.

"I was just enormously lucky," he said, "and that's all there is to say about it. In the last corner, about a kilometer before the finish, I reckoned on all or nothing and I took enormous risks. Normally I'd have hugged the curb. But this time I went right to the right and I came out of the bend flat out. And when I won, I told myself that that was it, that I was finished with racing. I had my eyes set on running a business."

"Enormously lucky" was Merckx's assessment as well. For him, the weather had been too good and his team too poor. It had given away too many chances to pure outsiders, so that Dolman won and the world's greatest came in anonymously in 76th.

Merckx carried on racing, of course, but Dolman retired soon afterward to work as an electrical repair man in Dordrecht. The reason he gave was a knee injury but the reality, says the Dutch chronicler, Fred van Slogteren, was that he was burned out. He went from doctor to doctor to find what made him feel weak, although one after the other told him there was nothing wrong and that it was in his head. He became serious and unsmiling. Cynics said the drugs had got to him.

"Slog" said: "Eef knew everything about cycling. His bike was no secret for him, he knew exactly how he reacted to whatever he ate and he had experimented with pills and needles so much that he knew when and where he had to use them. He had mastered everything, except that the UCI and the national bodies had decided to tackle doping. It cost him his national pro title in 1967 and the papers described him as hooked on wonder pills. Eef was nailed to the mast. The experience shattered him and, according to his wife, Sissy, he took nothing from then on."

Dolman died in hospital in 1993, aged 47. His Ronde, though, was the fastest, helped by an easier than usual course.

The spring of 1973 brought a new and, it has to be said, distinctive face to the Ronde. Belgian journalists tired of years of domination by Eddy Merckx seized on Freddy Maertens as the man to break their tedium. What new could be said of Merckx winning yet another race? And Maertens, overkeen and an uncomplicated lad unaware of the diplomacy a talented newcomer should show, put *les pieds dans le plat*. It's French for committing a tactless error.

Rik Vanwalleghem, his biographer, wrote: "He rode as he had as an amateur: straight to the front, fire in his belly, opposition in his gun sights. He couldn't see that in the world of grown-ups there were other, higher interests in play. His naïve joy in races and his fight for victory meant he didn't notice how many feathers he ruffled. He blundered without timidity into Merckx, the very emblem of cycling. And into De Vlaeminck. And into everyone else of the established order. Not to cause offense but through a youthful, natural enthusiasm that blinded him to the consequences. More social skills would have made the difference. But by then the damage was done; his rebellious intrusion had made him enemies."

He came second in Kuurne–Brussels–Kuurne, again in the Omloop der Vlaamse Ardennen, third in A Travers la Belgique, fifth in Gent–Wevelgem, fifth in Paris–Roubaix, eighth in the Amstel Gold Race. It was an insolence the established order didn't appreciate and it showed in 1973's Ronde.

Maertens was away towards the end with Merckx, Eric Leman and Willy De Geest. The finish had just moved to Meerbeke. But less obvious were the politics that went on before they got there. Merckx had just dumped Lomme Driessens as his team manager. The effective but self-aggrandizing Driessens had gone off to manage another team, Rokado. Its sponsor was a German company making mattress supports for beds.

Driessens didn't taking his firing kindly and was as keen that one of his riders should win as he was that Merckx shouldn't. He told De Geest to stay on Merckx's wheel and neutralize everything he did. He then suggested to Briek Schotte, the manager of Maertens' Flandria team, that De Geest ride for Maertens and lead him out in the sprint. De Geest couldn't outsprint Maertens, so he'd be no worse off, but leading out Maertens would guarantee his victory and at the same time deny Merckx. It wasn't a bad plan if you thought in those terms. But the connivance came at a price. And Schotte, never a big spender and feeling Maertens could win without help, wouldn't spend the money.

At the same time, Merckx was also plotting to stop Maertens. The newcomer hadn't showed respect and he was to be taught a lesson. The best lesson, of course, was that Merckx should win, which he couldn't do by outsprinting Maertens but might manage by breaking away alone. He watched over his shoulder as team cars came and went and their drivers negotiated through windows. Not knowing what arrangements were being made but feeling sure that he'd have been told had he been the planned beneficiary, he attacked and Leman went with him. Leman won, Merckx came third but, just as important in the small and petty world of Belgian cycling, Maertens came only second.

Maertens never did win the Ronde. But go to the race's museum in Oudenaarde and there in the wide street window you'll see bricks lettered with the name of each year's winner. The 1977 brick shows the race was won by Roger De Vlaeminck. And that is accurate. But above it is another, that reads: "Moral winner: Freddy Maertens." The brick's presence owes something to Maertens' role as curator there. De Vlaeminck is possibly less happy about it.

The 1977 race was on Sunday April 3, from the Grote Markt in Brugge to the Minderbroedersstraat in Oudenaarde, after 256 kilometers and 17 hills. De Vlaeminck recalled long afterwards in *Het Nieuwsblad* that the day had rain, wind and cold, "everything you needed to make a great Ronde."

De Vlaeminck was wearing the red, white and blue jersey of the Brooklyn team, sponsored by an Italian chewing gum maker and making prolific use of the American flag, even though the gum was never sold in the USA. Maertens was wearing the rainbow jersey of world champion that he had won the previous summer in Ostuni, Italy. Just before the start, race officials told team directors that riders would not be allowed to change bikes on or before the Koppenberg. The significance is that the Koppenberg is so steep and cobbled that bikes used for the rest of the course would not have sufficiently low gearing.

Freddy Maertens' team officials said they never received or never agreed to this decision, or at any rate that not all of them had. It is all hazy. Therefore Maertens took a new bike from Jef D'Hondt, his soigneur. D'Hondt said he gave it to Maertens because the team manager, Driessens, told him to. "The team managers had agreed before the start that there'd be no bike changes at the Koppenberg but Driessens didn't think that need apply to him. He was the boss and he did his own thing," he said.

Maertens insisted that something had gone wrong with his original bike and that therefore he needed a new one. It was an old ruse and it convinced nobody. And so, on a new bike with more suitable gearing, Maertens crested the Koppenberg and, with Roger De Vlaeminck, pushed on alone towards the finish.

What happened next depends on how you hear the story. All the versions end with Maertens staying in the race, whether he heard of his disqualification at the time or not, and that for 70 kilometers he dragged De Vlaeminck faster than their chasers could ride. "He rode that day as only Eddy Merckx could have ridden," De Vlaeminck acknowledged.

Both he and Maertens agree that money was to change hands. "That's normal," Maertens says, using one of his favorite expressions.

"And why didn't they take me out of the race from the start," he asks, referring to the commissaires. "Why? Because it would keep a better show for the TV, of course."

Maertens had done most of the work and covered most of the distance when a UCI commissaire, Jos Fabri, told him he was out of the race. Or, as Maertens remembered it, he said: "You can no longer qualify for first place [*gij telt niet meer winnen*]. He never said I had to get off. He never said I was disqualified."

Maertens and Fabri had never been friends. They had clashed because of Fabri's other role, which was chairman of the national racing committee and therefore Belgium's head team selector. Picking a Belgian team in those years was a diplomatic and business nightmare, few stars being prepared to ride for anyone else, each insisting he have his trade-team colleagues with him, each sponsor demanding a better slice of the deal. Maertens, in his permanent war with Merckx, and with Flandria being a cut-price sponsor compared to Merckx's backers, consistently felt he was given an unfair deal. And Fabri was the man he held responsible.

De Vlaeminck says he knew nothing of the bike change, although he did hear what Fabri shouted. He said that Maertens didn't slow down, especially after Driessens drove up beside him and yelled for him to stay in the race.

Only a handful of kilometers remained. Maertens kept going until, with 300 meters left, De Vlaeminck rose out of the saddle and sprinted down the left of the road. Maertens, too tired or not inclined to try,

Roger De Vlaeminck, a complicated man but brimming with class.

made no reaction. He crossed the line turning the pedals slowly and wiping his nose. Helpers rushed to grab De Vlaeminck and Maertens rode by without a glance.

"We never sprinted for the finish," De Vlaeminck said. "Freddy was shattered and worried about his disqualification. There was no cheering. I was proud to have won the Ronde at last but not of the way I'd done it." And Maertens was indeed disqualified. As he would have been anyway because of doubts about his dope test.

Maertens insists that De Vlaeminck heard Fabri's shouted remarks and that, because he knew Maertens wouldn't be allowed to win, he'd asked him to work for him and said: "I'll make it worth your while."

Maertens says: "I asked 150,000 francs for myself and 150,000 for my teammates. De Vlaeminck agreed. Before the Wall of Grammont he asked me to really get going. 'It's still 300,000 francs?', I asked. 'Ja, ja,' he said."

De Vlaeminck, says Maertens, gave him 150,000 francs while they were training together by the coast. Maertens gave it to Michel Pollentier and Marc Demeyer for their help in discouraging the chase. But he never saw the further 150,000 he expected for his own services. De Vlaeminck says they never discussed money—or at least the amount—and the argument has never closed, even if it has grown less passionate.

All the continent's reporters turned against De Vlaeminck and so did spectators at the finish. Including a fish dealer who pushed his way to De Vlaeminck at the finish and, his face close to De Vlaeminck's, screamed: "A beautiful Ronde…and you had to go and ruin it!" De Vlaeminck shrugged it off. And, in a country and a sport where passions flare and die, perhaps even forgot it. Two years passed. And then the fish man, a Maertens supporter, called De Vlaeminck at home to apologize and to ask how he could make amends.

"The man didn't owe me anything," De Vlaeminck explained later, "but he gave my brother, Erik, 20,000 francs to pass on to me to make things good again. Quite a fishmonger."

Second place is still shown as X. For a short moment the runner-up's place was credited to Maertens, because on the evening of the race Fabri told the press that "The race jury has come to the decision that Maertens was the victim of a mechanical defect. The illegal bike change had no influence on the result of the race, which can therefore stand as genuine. As a humane gesture the jury has decided that Freddy Maertens, in recognition of the remarkable athletic ability that he showed for 70 kilometers, will not be taken out of the result."

That wasn't the end of a curious race nor of Maertens' troubles. For a start, the directors of other teams felt cheated. They too could have changed their riders' bikes before the Koppenberg, but they hadn't. "It's going just too far," said Jan Raas' manager angrily. "The rules in a race as important as the Ronde van Vlaanderen are there to be respected by everyone."

The race had indeed been falsified, he insisted. De Vlaeminck would not have stayed away to the end had Maertens not been prepared to sell his own chances to see to it that he did. The race jury thought that a pretty good argument and changed its mind again. Maertens was back out of the race.

And was that the end? Well, no. Maertens tested positive at the drug check. So did Walter Planckaert, who had come third. And the Frenchman Guy Sibille was thrown out for not turning up at the check at all. Maertens won the Waalse Pijl a few days later... and was again disqualified. Lab technicians had found a way to detect Stimul, a popular amphetamine-like stimulant which until then riders had taken knowing it wouldn't show up in urine tests. Now it did. The Belgian and Italian cycling federations saw best not to pass this information to the riders—about which Maertens in his autobiography, *Niet Van Horen Zeggen* [Not From Hearsay], writes with great indignation— and the carnage included Maertens, Merckx and Walter Planckaert.

The self-awarded lettered brick in Oudenaarde is all that Maertens got. Cycling itself, though, became cleaner. Dr Jean-Pierre de Mondenard, the historian of sports doping and a former Tour de France doctor, said: "Professor Michel Debackere perfected a way to identify pemoline, part of the amphetamine family, a stimulant of the central nervous system, forbidden but until then undetectable. It was the end of an era. Of course, amphetamines carried on circulating in athletes' pockets, but it was risky and the elite turned progressively away from it, at least in races."

Such was Eddy Merckx's domination by 1975 that reporters at the finish gave more attention to Frans Verbeeck, who for 100 kilometers had clung to Merckx's wheel as De Vlaeminck had to Maertens'. Merckx was on a roll. It was the year in which he won Milan–San Remo for the sixth time, Liège–Bastogne–Liège for the fifth time, and the year-long Super Prestige Pernod (successor to the Desgrange-Colombo), which he had won every year from 1969. He was beaten only by Roger De Vlaeminck in Paris–Roubaix and came third behind André Dierickx and Verbeeck in the Flèche Wallonne. And now Verbeeck had the guts to stay with Merckx in the Ronde. Not, you'll notice, the guts to go past him—merely to cling on, powerless to do otherwise.

Merckx remembered: "I could hear Frans sighing and swearing. When we first got away, he took on some of the work now and then. But then it was finished." For hours Verbeeck clung to Merckx's wheel,

"All I could do was hang on", said Frans Verbeeck of Eddy Merckx, 1975.

his white Maes jersey matching the white with rainbow bands of Merckx's world championship colors. He had no more to give at Denderwindeke, with six kilometers to go, and Merckx shook him off.

He finished 30 seconds ahead of Verbeeck and more than five minutes before the first of the chasers.

Merckx gave calm and reflective interviews at the finish. The man who'd been on his wheel for 100 kilometers clung to a railing to keep his legs from buckling. Then Fred De Bruyne, who had won the race in 1957 and was by then an interviewer for Belgian television reputed to be loaded with drink before each broadcast, pushed his microphone into Verbeeck's drawn and grimy face. He asked for his reaction. Verbeeck spoke in short weary phrases. "I have to…tell it…like it is. He rode… five kilometers an hour…too fast for everyone." That afternoon he let his wife drive him home. He rarely allowed her to drive.

Verbeeck just didn't see the point in fighting Merckx. Like so many others, he won less because of him, his contract prices were reduced because of him. And in the words of Fred van Slogteren: "There just wasn't any more bread on the plate for him and, in contrast with other riders, he fancied doing something else." He earned so little in the peloton that he continued as he had as an amateur, delivering milk to houses in Wilsele, even on the morning before races. It brought him the nickname of the cycling milkman. So in June 1966 he decided that three years as a professional were enough and he stopped. He had won only seven races in four years. He went back to delivering milk.

Round the streets he went at dawn, placing bottles on doorsteps before Belgium was awake, doing a job he liked and understood. It was just so uncomplicated. Then he realized he still had legs at 27 and he came back after three years. He finally retired in 1978, to run a clothing company, having won 161 times during his comeback. Oddly, for a man who delivered milk, he rode almost always for companies making alcoholic drinks: Wiel's ("the beer of champions"), Okay Whisky, Geens (gin), and Watney and Maes, brewers.

Frustrated throughout by Merckx, he took the diplomatic and good-for-copy line that "There was nothing to be done and if I have to be second then I'm proud to be second behind Eddy."

How is it that people will do the impossible to be at a bike race? Why do they stand for hours in the rain and cold until they see a few riders flash by? You don't do that through logic; you do it for the magic. Maybe one day that atmosphere, that attraction, will be lost. That's what people have said ever since world war two. But still the people go and stand there. Maybe we have a greater need for the romantic than we're prepared to accept.

—Louis De Lentdecker, *Het Nieuwsblad*

7

A Race Of Men

There are days when nobody should be out on a bike. The first Sunday of April 1985 was one of them. It was bad enough as riders huddled for warmth in the glorious baroque square in St-Niklaas, where the race had moved in 1977. The wind bit with its coldness. It swept across an area only slightly less large than the Red Square in Moscow. And then at mid-distance of the race the clouds grew still blacker and broke, sending water sploshing across the roads and mud streaming over the cobbles.

Only 24 of the 173 riders made it to the finish. Rik Vanwalleghem said: "It was a legendary Ronde, one which wrote Sport with a capital S. It was as cold as Siberia all day and the rain fell in torrents. In this apocalyptic background Eric Vanderaerden got back to the front after looking beaten to ride 20 kilometers at the head of the race alone. Impressive."

L'Équipe in France called it "a race of men." It said: "From the Koppenberg onwards it was a race of man against man. In sport, that is always the most beautiful, the most authentic. There were no tactics. Luck and team managers didn't come into it. For the last two hours of the race I never saw [Vanderaerden's team manager] Peter Post. The extremes of the weather meant that, more than ever, the best won."

The story is that a group of around 40 led at ever greater speed as it approached what Vanderaerden calls "the witches' wall" of the Koppenberg. Not one of the 40 had overlooked the importance of the climb. And then, a few kilometers before the turning to the hill, Vanderaerden punctured. Ludo De Keulenaer gave him a wheel from his own bike—Vanderaerden has also said it was the red-haired

Dutchman, Bert Oosterbosch—and he set off again, paced by Johan Lammerts, wearing himself down, reaching the leaders on the first slopes.

"For me, it was a hopeless task," he said, "but I threw myself at it, a bit like a circus performer. I made up 15, 20 places and got a gap." He was helped by riders who, he said, had got off to walk "even though they weren't in difficulties." He could, he said, either feel sorry for his bad luck or he could give what he had. And he gave it.

"At that moment, nobody had reacted. I was by myself with 70 kilometers to go. What was I to do? I could sit up or I could give it full gas. I gave it gas and the gap held. But then Hennie Kuiper set off after me."

Hennie Kuiper, in his mid-30s and towards the end of a career that included a world championship, the 1981 Ronde and five stages of the Tour de France, went past him. He gained a minute and still there was no reaction. Vanderaerden waited as long as he dared for someone else to do the work, then turned to his teammate, a toothy Australian called Phil Anderson.

"Our turn to attack," Vanderaerden told him.

Anderson looked back at him.

"You first," he said.

Vanderaerden attacked on a hill at Brakel and Anderson followed him, which he hadn't expected. They reached Kuiper just before Geraardsbergen, or Grammont as it's known in French. On the southern edge of the town, after a drop down the main street and then a rise up the other side, is a dog-leg cobbled climb to a small chapel at the summit.

"I knew that was where the verdict would come," Vanderaerden said, "and I bust a gut and I won. I have to say that I'm proud of that, particularly because everyone had me down as a sprinter."

The attack brought a chilly encounter with Anderson, who thought he was the safer bet and also more deserving. He had won the Amstel Gold Race in 1983 but he needed another big win. Vanderaerden didn't see it that way. He was a Belgian in his own land and nothing could beat a win in Belgium's most prestigious race.

"He had good legs that day as well," he said. "But I was first up the Tenbossche and I was first up the Wall of Grammont. End of discussion."

Vanderaerden's career declined after 1988 and he retired eight years later to manage minor professional teams. Anderson retired to what he calls the life of a gentleman farmer in Jamieson, Victoria, where the idea of running an Australian professional team is never low in his thoughts.

It was on the Bosberg rather than the Koppenberg that the big moment came for Edwig van Hooydonck, or "Eddy" to friends. This thin-faced, sometimes anemic-looking man with bright red hair, married to Raymond Poulidor's daughter, was born in Ekeren, a

Edwig van Hooydonck, 1991: "I bust a gut and I won."

northern suburb of Antwerp. It's beside the docks and just north of where the city's indoor track used to be. On April 7, 1991, this *Antwerpenaar* with the difficult accent to match earned the nickname Eddy Bosberg.

Van Hooydonck wasn't the strongest but the rest were wary of him. Two years earlier, at 22 he had won the Ronde, sobbing on the podium.

And in the winter, he said, he had trained 80 or 90 times round the route, including the Bosberg. Even now he can point to the concrete telephone pole where he attacked, the second on the left, a yellow metal band showing it as number 1050. In 1989 he countered an attempt by Dag-Otto Lauritzen and then attacked on the left of the road, hands grasping the flat top of his handlebars, his body bobbing with effort. His yellow and black Superconfex jersey, never one of cycling's most attractive, was spattered with mud and sweat and rain.

He crossed the summit alone. There were 13 kilometers to go, the rain pouring, lines of spectators creating a three-meter corridor all the way to the finish. He climbed to the podium and his face, thinner then than now and the hair a little redder, twisted in uncontrollable tears.

In 1991, then, the others watched for him but couldn't believe he had benefited from anything but surprise and good luck two years earlier. They had forgotten his reputation for alternating his seasons, first a good one, then nothing, then another good one. So in 1991 he was due for another good one. And the Sunday before the Ronde he won the Flèche Brabançonne.

Van Hooydonck went to the start of the Ronde that year uncertain how far he would get. He had an inflamed calf and hadn't trained much all week, afraid hot stabbing pains would return during the race. But they didn't and pretty soon, as the others failed to dislodge him, and as the favorites repeatedly split and regrouped on the climbs, they began to see the risk he represented.

Van Hooydonck had the nickname Eddy Bosberg, but nobody thought the same tactic and the same place could work twice. Yet it did. Van Hooydonck attacked soon after Brakel and took with him the Dane, Rolf Sørensen, followed by Johan Museeuw and a German, Rolf Gölz. They all now realized what van Hooydonck planned: another attack on the Bosberg. But expect it as they might, they could neither stop its happening nor its succeeding. He won by 45 seconds.

At the finish he said: "It was a lot harder today than two years ago. In 1989 I was almost unknown; today I was one of the favorites. And that changes everything."

Van Hooydonck rode the Ronde again, coming third in 1992, seventh in 1993 and ninth in 1994. In 1996, still not 30, he left the sport, saying he wasn't prepared to take the blood-enhancer, EPO, like so many others.

As an aside, van Hooydonck was another with the magic number 9. Every winner since the end of world war two who won in a year ending in 9 has won the race at least twice. Fiorenzo Magni won in 1949, 1950 and 1951; Rik van Looy won in 1959 and 1962; Eddy Merckx in 1969 and 1975; Jan Raas in 1979 and 1983; van Hooydonck in 1989 and 1991; Peter van Petegem in 1999 and 2003; and Stijn Devolder in 2008 and 2009.

But to some, even in Belgium, van Hooydonck's wins were good to watch but not worthy of the Ronde. Nor was Belgium worthy of its race. Belgians won five times from 1990 to 2000. But, equally, that means foreigners won the other half. And that had never happened in the history of the race, although the 1980s pointed the way with four foreign wins.

In its way, it was no worse than was happening in the Tour de France. Cycling had become more international, which meant more riders and more foreigners. But the new Ronde winners weren't from eastern Europe or another continent. They were from the established nations. Belgium had declined even among its peers.

Frank Vandenbroucke saw an explanation: "The mid-1990s [were] a dark period for Belgian cycling. Apart from the then still unassuming Lotto, there wasn't a Belgian professional team worthy of the name. GB-MG was Italian-Belgian but it was based in Italy. And below those two there was a big gap. We hadn't done anything for decades in big stage races and we even got trounced in our own races at home by the armada of stronger riders from abroad. We owed our cycling fame to the seventies and the glory days of Eddy Merckx and we thought it would all come good again. And every day we praised ourselves as the giants of cycling, we lost more and more ground to Italian and Spanish teams who'd made big advances in equipment, training methods and medical treatment."

In 1992 the whole field was belittled. Jacky Durand these days is a skilled and entertaining television commentator, bringing insight and humor alternately. As a rider, he was so known for long and frequently suicidal attacks that the magazine *Vélo* instituted a Jackymetre to display just how many kilometers he had ridden alone. In 2001, for instance, it showed he had raced 16,524 kilometers and been in breaks for 2,270 kilometers of them.

"I've spent my whole career knowing I'll never win the Tour," he said in 2000, "so I rely on my media value. If I do something, it gets in the papers. Sometimes, 100 kilometers of riding alone in the Tour de France has more significance than a win in another race."

There were just the usual amused smiles, then, when Dudu—French for a teddybear—set off by on the morning of Sunday April 5, 1992, and rode into the distance. Durand had won Tour stages that way but he had lost far more. And a Frenchman hadn't won the Ronde for 36 years, so why worry?

Durand had been with Thomas Wegmüller, Patrick Roelandt and Hervé Meyvisch, none of them names to excite the heart. Durand, just 25, was unknown in Belgium. And, beneath the uninterested eyes of the favorites, the minnows got a lead of more than 22 minutes. Drawing them along was the Swiss, Wegmüller, winner of the Grand Prix des Nations time trial in 1990 and second in Paris–Roubaix in 1988 but without much of record otherwise.

A handful of riders began to worry at their lead, particularly Johan Museeuw and van Hooydonck, but by then it was too late and Wegmüller too strong. Museeuw said: "It was one of those crazy things that happen. Usually, when something like that happens, the team leaders or the team captains take control of events. Now there are so many languages in the peloton that everyone looks the other way. And that included me. I didn't have the authority with the Lotto team then to be its captain. I didn't have the sway to be able to tell the team to get chasing. Well, it's a lesson learned."

There was hope when the break began to disintegrate, but no amount of chasing could bring it back. Just Durand and Wegmüller survived on the Bosberg and then Durand was alone. He finished 48 seconds ahead of the Swiss and 1 minute 44 seconds of a small chasing group led by van Hooydonck.

"I'd never thought of the Ronde as a race I could win," he said after thrusting both arms to the sky and crossing the line with a shout. "It was inaccessible. I didn't think I could win it, in 1992 or in any other year. I didn't even dream of it. It was the second time I'd ridden it and, the first time, I'd dropped out at the first feeding point. I could imagine winning Paris–Roubaix or Milan–San Remo but the Ronde was simply out of reach for someone like me. It's harder than Paris–Roubaix. There are the bad cobbles just as there in Roubaix but there are also those hills in succession.

"When I attacked, it wasn't to win. It was to survive! I just wanted to finish. At that moment, my ambition was above all to avoid riding up the Oude Kwaremont with all the peloton. I knew there'd be a lot of

Jacky Durand, 1992: great storyteller, great Ronde winner.

pushing and shoving there. I wanted to get there with a bit of a lead, say five or six minutes. But at the foot of the climb we had not five minutes but twenty. That changed a lot of things but I still didn't think of winning. Twenty minutes is enough in a lot of races. But not in the Ronde. They can come back to you very fast when the big guys get rolling."

The first time he thought he could win was when he dropped Wegmüller on the Bosberg.

"The problem was that we weren't being told how much lead we had, what the gaps were. All we knew was that van Hooydonck and Fondriest had attacked. What little else we were told was often contradictory. So we no longer knew if we had one minute's lead, two or even three. And at the end of a race, when you've ridden 200 kilometers in a break, you ride a lot slower than guys like van Hooydonck.

"Then, with five kilometers to go, Eddy Merckx came up alongside when I was by myself. He said: 'Son, you're going to win the Ronde.' And then I realized. I said to myself: 'Jacky, you've just pulled off the hold-up of the century.'"

Museeuw regretted his own position but he could see it another way as well. "It had a good side," he said. "The attackers got paid for their trouble. And why shouldn't they? The sun shines for everyone. And certainly for a rider as aggressive as Durand."

Mostly, the Ronde goes smoothly, remarkably so given the twisting, doubling nature of the route. But things weren't like that in 1994. A rider in the Banesto team crashed at Ingooigem and held up the procession of cars following the race. The five sag wagons, collectors of riders who've had enough, lost their police escort. The drivers set off in chase only to be sent the wrong way along with a line of spectators' cars. A search then began for the best way out of the streets of Kluisbergen, where they ended up.

The drivers, going faster than they dared, hadn't bargained on two cycle-tourists going the same way. Braking hard to avoid them, one of the buses slid into the ditch in Broektestraat, which is wide enough only for one vehicle. That was problem enough. But then the entourage realized they weren't behind the race but ahead of it, that the riders were about to swarm into the same road. Two tractors were enlisted to pull the bus from the ditch. But it wouldn't budge.

Jacquis De Winne, the head of the race caravan, drove at "full gas", as he put it, as soon as he got the news. Organizers and police halted the team cars that had correctly followed the race and the riders squeezed by the stranded buses. The stranded bus was eventually retrieved from the ditch and the sag wagons could make their way back to the race followers—to the applause, sometimes ironic, of all they passed.

In 1998, the race changed. For decades it had been a loop or an open square. It had started in the east and ridden towards the west. Now it was to be a one-way ride, starting not in St-Niklaas but far to the west in Brugge. The contract with St-Niklaas had ended and the Ronde was wooed back to its roots by Brugge, a city anxious to be more than a living museum. Brugge is the prettiest city in Belgium and draws millions of tourists. But the mayor, Patrick Moenaert, wanted a living city that traded on more than its looks. Having his city seen on television around the world could bring in industry and employment.

The move wasn't to everyone's taste, of course. Fer Schroeders lamented: "On the main square at St-Niklaas, at the foot of the magnificent city hall, the start of the Ronde was always a privileged moment. The riders came there to sign the start sheet before going down into the crowd to meet fans, not hesitating to sign a few autographs, posing for a souvenir photograph for a young admirer. Now there are fences to keep the public away from riders. The start of the Ronde van Vlaanderen has clearly lost, in this new configuration, everything that gave it its charm."

But there was also no shortage of enthusiasm. The crowd at that first start in Brugge was estimated at 15,000, packed so close that the man supposed to drop the flag couldn't push through them. Now, from Brugge, the Ronde rides along the North Sea coast from Knokke-Heist before turning diagonally across the country to reach the classic hills before riding on to the established finish at Meerbeke.

That year the race lost more than some of its charm. It lost Rudy Dhaenens, an improbable world champion in 1990 but a world champion nevertheless. Dhaenens—pronounced *Dah-n'ns*—came second in the Ronde that same year, a poor sprinter beaten in a two-man sprint by Moreno Argentin. Getting on the podium but rarely its top rung was characteristic of his career. As a result, said the American writer, Sam Abt: "Usually he looked like a small boy who asked Santa for a set of trains for Christmas and got instead underwear and a book. Dhaenens never had much luck."

Driving to the finish of the Ronde in 1998, to describe the race on the TV channel Eurosport, he lost control of his car on the E40 trans-European highway, skidded and hit an electricity pylon. He died the following day, aged 36. That year, Johan Museeuw won the Ronde for the first of three times. News of Dhaenens' death saddened him. "What does this win mean?" he asked at the press conference. "We should just be pleased that we can get out of bed again in the morning, have breakfast and drink coffee."

Museeuw comes from Gistel, a not especially beautiful town which forms the southerly point of a lopsided triangle created with Oostend and Brugge. It was the home of Sylvère Maes—prononounced *Maahce*—winner of the Tour de France in 1936 and 1939 and, in retirement, *patron* of the Café Tourmalet in the town. It's still there, little changed on the outside, at a junction of the main highway and the road to Nieuwpoort. The inside is decorated with pictures of Maes and with Museeuw's jerseys.

Museeuw would have been a successor to Eddy Merckx had he been able to ride stage races and, in particular, in their mountains. Instead, he had a talent for single-day races, winning the Ronde in 1998, 1995 and 1993, Paris–Roubaix in 2002, 2000 and 1996 and the world road race in 1996. But success in the Ronde wasn't instant. He could have

Bugno and Museeuw duke it out at the finish in 1994.

won in 1994, and there are still fans who believe he did. He sprinted against the Italian, Gianni Bugno, close enough that their elbows could have touched. Centimeters before the line, Bugno was confident enough that he had won that he threw both arms in the air. And they were just coming down again as the two crossed the line.

Look at the photo finish even now and it's impossible to see which has won. The Belgian federation's picture, taken from the left of the road, shows Museeuw nearest the camera. Somehow, the judges decided Bugno had won, by about a third the width of his front tire. There was uproar from the crowd, which had seen the sprint only from behind or in front but which was determined a Belgian should win. But the judges held fast.

Museeuw's philosophical view was that "there really are worse things in life than losing the Ronde." And, anyway, he said, he had only himself to blame. He had ridden a faultless race right up to the last 500 meters. "For 269 kilometers everything I did was perfect," he mused. He had done whatever he wanted. But perhaps then confidence was replaced by doubt. Franco Ballerini started the sprint from a long way out but died at 250 meters. Museeuw, not knowing what to do, hesitated. He had depended on Ballerini as his springboard.

"And then I saw Bugno go, to my left. I immediately lost two lengths on him. There was no way I could make that up, not on the Bugno of those days. I should have gone as soon as Ballerini died. Shame, losing like that, but there's nothing to be done," he said years later. "All you can do is get on with the next task, look forward. Where's the sense in letting it gnaw away at you? I didn't even feel guilty for the team. They knew that I'd done all I could, they knew how winning and losing go together. In the last six years I've never said 'sorry' after a defeat. If you race at a high level, you have to be able to take the blows, to bounce back mentally."

In each Ronde until then, he acknowledged, he had made a mistake.

And then, in 1993, he got it right. And it happened on one of the more insignificant hills, in Tenbosschestraat ("To the wood street", in pre-reformed spelling, or Tenbossestraat as it's often written now) in Brakel. And, although he insists it was chance, it was on the same hill that he made his winning moves in 1995 and 1998. There were 177 starters, setting off from St-Niklaas in light rain that ended after an hour. There were the usual early attacks, breaks and collapses and then the decision came with 75 kilometers to go.

There, on the Tiegemberg, the stars went to the front. Edwig van Hooydonck was there, Frans Maassen, Franco Ballerini, Johan Museeuw and a handful of others. Museeuw attacked on the light hill through Brakel and only Maassen stayed with him.

Maassen was a not insignificant companion. He won the Tour of Belgium in 1988, his second year as a professional, the Dutch road championship in 1989, the Tour of Belgium again in 1990, the Amstel Gold Race and the Tour of Holland in 1991, and the Three Days of De Panne just before the Ronde in 1992. He had also won the red jersey for the greatest number of intermediate sprints in the Tour de France.

Maassen, however, had no interest in helping Museeuw, not simply because he was Dutch and Museeuw Belgian or even because they rode for different teams. He simply wasn't going to help, even though his power as a time-trialist would have been invaluable and his ability as a sprinter—remember that red jersey for Tour primes—could have given Museeuw a good challenge.

Whatever the calculations that went through his head, he decided either that he was going to save his strength for the sprint at the end, or that the time could come when he could ride away alone, or even that their attack wasn't going to succeed and that he'd save himself until

Johan Museeuw denies Frans Maassen in 1993.

other riders caught them and made their group more substantial. And he stayed where he was, on Museeuw's wheel.

"It was a real pain," Museeuw remembered. "Maassen wouldn't come through. I rode kilometer after kilometer at the front."

That left Museeuw with no option but to surrender and let the the others catch him or to plow on and suffer whatever Maassen inflicted at the end. The situation infuriated Museeuw's gray-haired and wine-loving team manager, Patrick Lefevère. And then, finally, on the Wall of Grammont within reach of the finish at Meerbeke, Maassen saw "the ridiculousness of the situation", as Museeuw put it, and joined in with the work.

Museeuw denied they ever talked of money. He said Maassen just began to believe in his chance of winning and wanted to stay clear. Equally Maassen knew that Edwig van Hooydonck was trying to get up to them and that, two against one, he had far less chance of success. But Maassen never did win; the two finished 22 seconds ahead of the rest with the Dutchman on the Belgian's wheel.

Maassen went on to manage the Rabobank team in Holland and had the novelty of advising riders on the race he had so narrowly lost.

"All the Belgians on the Wall of Grammont were swearing at me," he recalled, "calling me a dirty Dutchman and spitting at me. And then suddenly I began riding a bit better. I thought that maybe I did have a chance against Museeuw. You have to remember that he was Belgian champion that year and as much a favorite as Tom Boonen would be now. It's true that I hadn't done as much work at the front but van Hooydonck couldn't make the jump up to us. So the two of us stayed in the lead. Museeuw won the sprint really easily. Afterwards, I still felt good about it. Because I'd done everything I had to do. It was simply that I got to the finish with a man who was faster than I was."

Two years later, 1995, Museeuw won again, this time in the startling jersey of the Mapei team. The rag-doll patchwork of Mapei jerseys gave ample ammunition to those who felt that cycling clothes could get no more over-complicated or tasteless. The year that Museeuw won for the second time was the season in which Frank Vandenbroucke joined the team, on the very day of the Ronde. Vandenbroucke in his autobiography remembered a conversation in front of the television in his family's bar near the French border, at Ploegsteert:

"All those colors mixed up together. Those Mapei-GB jerseys are a mess, aren't they?"

"I was told Squinzi's wife designed them."

"Who?"

"Squinzi, the boss of Mapei, a building company."

"I hope his buildings look better than his jerseys."

"Maybe that's why they win so much. They want to get to the finish as fast as they can to put something else on."

Roars of laughter.

Museeuw attacked in that dazzle-camouflage jersey on the same hill in Brakel. And then once more in 1998, his third win. In 1995 he missed the break after puncturing, regained it, then attacked. By the top of the Wall of Grammont he was alone, riding on to win by just short of a minute and a half. And much the same happened in 1998, Museeuw regaining ground on the break, passed the last escapee on the Tenbosschestraat and cruised in alone with 43 seconds' lead.

Things didn't go as well after that. He fell in Paris–Roubaix a week later; infection set in in his injured leg and he came close to losing it. Two years later he fell again in a motorcycle accident. His relief at racing again showed when, on winning Paris–Roubaix in 2000, he pointed to his lifted leg to show how well it had healed.

And then things grew worse again in his last season and during retirement. Rumors that he had taken drugs led to their confirmation and a 10-month suspended jail sentence.

The worst thing about cobbles is that it's hard to hold someone's wheel, to stick with them. On cobbles, you can't profit from speed. You have to keep pushing hard just to keep the same speed. Above all, you have to concentrate. You're so occupied with the cobbles that you barely see the rest of the race. It's even worse if the cobbles are wet. You have to have the strength. But above all it's a matter of mentality.

—Roger De Vlaeminck, winner 1977

8

Into Modern Times

In 1999, Peter van Petegem made the most of a pile-up just before the Wall of Grammont at Geraardsbergen. It rises gently rise through the village, the riders slung into it by the descent that precedes it, then turns to the left and rises on cobbles to a chapel at the summit. Until the middle of the last century, the road through the town was also cobbled; now it's only the hill itself.

Were it not for the cobbles, the Wall would be just another stiff climb. And, even with the cobbles, Sunday enthusiasts can get up it, even the difficult left-hand bend a few hundred meters before the top. But those weekend riders aren't racing and they haven't already ridden more than 200 kilometers. For anyone who is and who has, the Wall is the final indignity in a race threaded with them.

The race in 1999 had covered almost 250 kilometers when it reached the Wall and van Petegem attacked with Johan Museeuw. Frank Vandenbroucke, a disturbed rider who died young in an African hotel, got up to them. Van Petegem remembered: "I was sure I'd win. After the Bosberg, the last hill, there were three of us at the front: Museeuw, Vandenbroucke and me. There was no time to hesitate since the pack were only 20 seconds behind. But then hesitating is never an option at the Ronde. Anyway, that race finished in a sprint. Museeuw was still suffering that year with a knee injury [after his crash in Paris–Roubaix] so I know I could beat him easily, and Vandenbroucke had been showing himself at the front all day. I was quite sure of the win."

And he won. Vandenbroucke came second and Museeuw third. Only 70 more of the 189 starters crossed the line behind them.

Van Petegem rode almost every Ronde from 1993 until he retired in 2007. He knew straight away it was his race, he says, and that one day he would win. But in 2002: "I was so sure that I would win and I

Peter van Petegem, 1999: "You have to love cobbles."

hesitated too long. I lost. That was by far my biggest misjudgment in the Tour of Flanders. The Ronde is all about timing and luck." He called Andrea Tafi "a lucky dog" for winning that year.

Tafi, of course, probably saw it differently. He attacked too often for his win to owe much to luck. In fact the reporter Tim Maloney likened him to "the battery bunny", a reference to a television advertisement of the period in which a toy rabbit powered by the advertiser's batteries went on and on while the rest faded.

Van Petegem got his glory in 2003, clapping his hands above his head as Vandenbroucke freewheeled several meters behind him with his head drooped. "No one could beat me," he said. "No one." His moment came through Brakel, where he was born and where for years there were cartoon portraits of him beside the course. "That was moment, on the Tenbosse, and I did it. Only Vandenbroucke could follow me, but I was certain I'd win in the sprint. I wanted to attack on the Tenbosse in 1998, too. I countered an attack from my teammate,

Ghendrik van Dijck, but it was Museeuw who attacked first. I reacted. The gap was five meters but I couldn't close it. Museeuw took advantage of the motorbikes in front of him and I cracked. Too bad. Under normal circumstances we'd have battled it out together."

Van Petegem—often described in the English-language cycling press as a giant but in fact simply 1 meter 77 (5' 10") and a lightweight, for all his stockiness, at 72 kilograms (159 pounds)—said: "I'm a cobblestone rider. You have to love cobbles. When I was at school and I cycled from my home in Brakel to Ninove, I rode the Wall of Grammont and the Bosberg every day. Later, I climbed the Molenberg ten times in a row. That was my passion."

He retired in 2007. He rides now for the fun of it, stopping to enjoy views he never saw in races, running a bike-touring company for those who want to ride with a former winner, and helping his wife, Angélique Segaert (women in Belgium are known formally by their maiden name), with their bed-and-breakfast near Sint-Maria-Horebeke. Their house is called Le Pavé, French for "the cobbles", which acknowledges his victory in Paris–Roubaix in 2003.

It's Angélique's rather than her husband's project. Van Petegem himself went into selling insurance when he climbed off his bike. And with one of those enjoyable twists of history, he became race director of the Omloop Het Nieuwsblad, a race he won three times (1997, 1998 and 2002) under its original name of the Omloop Het Volk.

Just as a footnote, and perhaps even as a warning, Le Pavé is not an inexpensive place to stay. It can cost up to €250 a night.

Then, as ever, came another face, a man who was the giant that van Petegem, physically, never was. *Tommeke*, they called him in Flanders, *-ke* being a dimunitive, like Johnny for John. It was partly the familiarity that fans feel for their heroes but it was also a joke: Tom Boonen is 1 meter 92 (6' 4") tall. Belgians aren't a tall nation and that's 16 centimeters taller than the Belgian average.

Boonen comes from outside Antwerp rather than from West or East Flanders, the heartland of Belgian cycling. He speaks Dutch with the harsh accent of the city, although he also speaks fluent French and English. A characterful man who soon made himself popular, he was nevertheless a troubled hero, caught three times after taking cocaine.

It dented his popularity in Belgium a little, along with his move to the tax haven of Monaco for a few years, but by then there had been enough other scandals in Belgium that what Boonen did in his spare time was soon forgotten.

Boonen won the Ronde in 2005, 2006 and 2012. In 2005 he rode away from the six riders left in the lead, pedaling with his characteristic flat-footed style, and won by 35 seconds. It answered doubters who pointed out that he'd never ridden such a distance in those conditions, that the Ronde wasn't Gent–Wevelgem or the Prix E3, other races he'd won.

That year's race started with a silence, not for the lambs about to be led to Boonen's slaughter but for Pope John Paul II, who'd died on April 2.

Andreas Klier, a German, was never among the favorites—Freddy Maertens said on Belgian TV that morning that everyone was speaking of Fabian Cancellara but that personally he would never rule out Boonen—but he rode as though he was. Class shows, though, or the lack of it, and he faded. When he did, van Petegem attacked, nine kilometers from the finish at Meerbeke. Boonen followed, van Petegem eased—and Boonen took off alone.

The chase that followed was an epic. Five seconds is not a lot at the end of a classic, and the classic, at that, that Belgians all want to win. But Boonen held it, increased it by a further 20 seconds as the others hesitated to chase for fear of losing second place as well as first, and Boonen had the confidence to sit up on the Halsesteenweg in Meerbeke and salute the crowd. Klier, whose move had been the catalyst, came in second, 35 seconds behind Boonen and 5 ahead of van Petegem. Winning for a third time equaled the record of Achiel Buysse, Fiorenzo Magni, Eric Leman and Johan Museeuw.

That year Boonen won not just the Ronde but Paris–Roubaix and the world championship. That did it. Next year—2006—the king himself turned up. Albert II was never one of the world's more flamboyant monarchs and the way the cameras kept returning to a silver-haired, bespectacled man who looked like a retired family doctor puzzled viewers around the world until a caption arrived to explain who he was. This was the 90th Ronde and Albert realized he was unlikely to be there for the 100th, or at any rate not willing to brave the weather. He was already 71 and feeling unwell. Seven years later he told parliament he didn't have the health to continue and he abdicated.

That warm day in 2006, though, he put on a raincoat and sat in the stand in Halsesteenweg and watched Boonen outsprint a lugubrious fellow Belgian called Leif Hoste.

Hoste, with bags under his eyes and with sallow cheeks that surround a full and drooping mouth, was the most miserable-looking rider in Belgium since Rudy Dhaenens—the man, you remember, of whom Sam Abt said: "He looked like a small boy who asked Santa for

Tom Boonen, larger than life in every sense, tackles the Grammont.

a set of trains for Christmas and got instead underwear and a book." He had reason to look depressed.

Hoste attacked on the Valkenberg and he and Boonen had shared the effort of staying away until their rivalry returned in the last few hundred meters. Hoste was never going to win. The best he could do was finish without shame.

"My bad luck was to get away with a far stronger rider," he told reporters despondently.

That would be enough for one man. But then came Paris–Roubaix and Hoste again finished second—only to be disqualified along with others who'd ridden through a closed train crossing.

That bad luck continued. The next year, 2007, he was outsprinted in the Ronde by Alessandro Ballan, a lanky Italian known as *Bontempino* for his resemblance to Guido Bontempi, a rider of the previous generation who won 16 stages of the Giro and 6 of the Tour de France. It was a flattering nickname, unlike *Elephantino* for wingnut-eared Marco Pantani, his fellow countryman.

Hoste animated the race once more, but this time leaving it until the Wall at Geraardsbergen. Again, just one rider went with him: Ballan. And again Hoste realized he was with a stronger sprinter, for a while slowing to force the Italian to the front. That worked but it almost failed because his chicanery let the chasers close to a handful of seconds. Then the two came to their senses and gambled no more. Hoste knew he couldn't win but tried nevertheless, sprinting to Ballan's left. But it was no good. Ballan's everyday job was to lead out sprints for Daniele Bennati and lead-out men are sometimes faster than their masters. Hoste stood no chance.

The Belgian's first reaction at the finish was politely reported by some as "*Verdomme*", a tactful contraction of a word that doesn't sound like much in English but is pretty pungent in Dutch. Other reports suggest a good command of international invective and insist he said "Fuck! *Godverdomme!*" He'd also fallen off twice. "No wonder I felt so bad," he snapped.

He played the role of Miserable Loser as though Shakespeare had written it for him. And life never did get better. He retired at the end of 2012, by which time he had descended to one of those Belgian teams that not even Belgians can remember. Life should have been peaceful. He expected to ride out his career in consoling obscurity and then perhaps to open a bar or a garage or trade on what reputation remained to get an office job somewhere. Instead, the country's cycling administrators demanded a fine of €300,000 after being alerted to a doping investigation by the UCI.

A succession of two-man sprints in the Ronde ended thanks to another Belgian, Stijn Devolder, in 2008. He had one of the most difficult first names in the peloton for English speakers. That *ij*—the digraph that is the unofficial 27th letter of the Dutch alphabet since the two characters are rightly joined together—makes a diphthong that sounds like *ay-ee*. So Devolder's first name is pronounced rather like *Stain*. He comes from Kortrijk—*Kor-tray-eek*—the city on the French border near Lille and Roubaix where Hoste lived and where, incidentally, Greg LeMond used to live. And, there, Devolder restored local pride. He rode away by himself for the last 30 kilometers in 2008, punching rather than turning the pedals, holding off a chase by a Dutchman, Sebastian Langeveld.

Langeveld never did win the Ronde but he did break his collar bone in the race in 2012, when he ran into a spectator. The bunch was swarming across the road for a sprint. Langeveld and another rider took their chance by switching to a bike path two or three meters from the right of road, going behind a sparse crowd. Spectators standing between the path and the road stepped back as the bunch threatened to overwhelm them. One went further and, not expecting riders to come from behind him, stepped back on to the path. His leg caught Langeveld's front wheel and the Dutchman fell on his right shoulder, snapping a bone.

In 2009, Devolder won again and added still more to Leif Hoste's miseries. Hoste got into a six-man group that got clear with 50 kilometers to go. He could at least hope for second place. But there with him was the toothy Frenchman, Sylvain Chavanel, whose main interest was to do nothing to hinder a chase by his team leader, Tom Boonen. Chavanel, highly rated in France but more hope than outstanding record, was a cautious homebird. Patrick Lefèvre had offered him a place in the team, as a talented domestique who'd be allowed his chance when it came, but Chavanel had hesitated. Not because he doubted the advantages of riding for Lefèvre…but because he worried about his pension. Would several years of foreign employment hinder his old age?

It took newspapers to remind him that European law allowed him to work wherever he chose within the EU and that his pension contributions would be respected. Chavanel then signed.

That year, Boonen and Italian Filippo Pozzato were the favorites. Wherever one went, the other would go too, crocodiles following Captain Hook. And, with Devolder, they rode up to the Hoste-Chavanel group.

Chavanel may have been put out because he had been surrendered to his stronger team-mate. But Hoste was even more upset. He was now outnumbered, with Chavanel, Boonen and Devolder all in the same team, sponsored by the Quick Step flooring company. Boonen was the best of the three but, by design or chance, it was Devolder who left the rest on the Wall at Geraardsbergen. He won by one second less than a full minute. The rest of the Boonen group slowed and was swallowed up by the peloton and the bunch crossed the line shaken by a crash in the last two hundred meters.

Boonen could be pleased that a teammate had won, Chavanel was less pleased because it hadn't been him, and Hoste wasn't pleased at all.

Geraardsbergen decided the Ronde again in 2010, and once more Boonen was a catalyst. He and a dark-haired and multi-lingual Swiss called Fabian Cancellara (he once modeled clothing and the Australian, Stuart O'Grady, teased that Cancellara was always late out of the shower after Paris–Roubaix "because of all his hair products") had been clear of the field for 40 kilometers. They were the strongest on the Molenberg and the race was over, other than deciding which would win.

Boonen had once been the world's strongest. Now he was weaker, less predictable and, worse, had a rival just as strong. Cancellara was one of the world's strongest in solo flight and he had won the previous season's world time-trial championship. Boonen would win in a sprint, both knew. So Cancellara had to rely on his strength and try to ride alone.

The two started the gentle lower slope of the Wall together. The approach road is signposted all through town. Two thirds of the way up walls of spectators, balanced on earth embankments, wait beside the cobbles to see bloodshed. They are the spectators like a blood clot waiting to burst, you'll remember. There, as the cobbles turned left, the gradient suddenly increased enough to break a man. And Cancellara knew it.

It was there that he tested Boonen and found there was no answer. Cancellara had a dozen seconds by the time he looped round two sides of the chapel at the summit. Boonen was too weak to do more. The Belgian's head sank as the difference between the two rose to a minute and a quarter. Cancellara used the invincible strength and flat-backed style that once spread claims that he had an electric motor hidden between his cranks. Nobody knows who nicknamed him Spartacus but it said a lot for his strength.

Since 2004 there has been a Ronde for women, a shorter race which partly precedes the men's. Typically, it is 127 kilometers long—half the men's distance—over 10 climbs and two stretches of flat cobbles. It attracts many of Europe's best riders but the range in their standard is greater than for the men. Many of those taking part are club riders, spear-carriers making up the field. Marianne Vos, the Dutch multiple world champion who won in 2013, says that fewer than a dozen women racers who call themselves professionals can actually make a living from cycling. The others are paid too little and win too little to support themselves without another job. There are therefore fewer professionals than sponsored amateurs. The consequence is that the women's Ronde is often a race not of attacks but of attrition: the best riders lead until the weakest have dropped off.

The outcome, especially since the women's race is on the same day as the men's, is that the *Vrouwenronde* gets less coverage than the women feel they deserve. Apart from anything else, to write more, newspapers would have to send twice as many reporters, which few could afford even if they felt inclined.

In 2013, the bespectacled mayor of Oudenaarde, Marnic de Meulemeester—who was also a member of the Flemish government— thought things had gone too far. Or, at any rate, not far enough. And he spoke out, although his opening words more or less explained how the situation had arisen.

"Although over recent years there has been a noticeable improvement,"—which acknowledges that the women's race wasn't all it might have been—"women's cycling is reported to the public far less. For example, the sporza.be website gives you almost nothing. A report of barely two minutes over Gent–Wevelgem for women and just 26 seconds over the women's version of the Omloop Het Nieuwsblad. And we read absolutely about Dwars door Vlaanderen."

National television had a duty to show more, he said. If it did that, women's racing would be more attractive to sponsors and the professional level of women's racing would grow. But for the moment, little has changed. The blogger, Sarah Connolly, said that same year: "People have been asking me how they can watch this race, and I've got some bad news to start with—there's no live TV, and if past years are anything to go by, it'll be very, very limited video coverage. Belgian TV station Sporza should show some short highlights of it after the men's race (maybe before the men's podium ceremony, maybe afterwards)—and this will be on their videozone after the race. In some years, they've cut to the women's finish line live in the men's coverage, but don't get your hopes up too much."

The most prolific winner is the German, Judith Arndt, who began as a world-class track pursuiter—third in the 1996 Olympics—and moved to the road. There she won the world championship in 2004 and came second in the Olympic Games of the same year.

In 2013 the organizers put the Molenberg at just short of 40 kilometers, which started the attrition early. But then the difference in standards showed even more prominently on the two and a half kilometers of the Oude Kwaremont. Marianne Vos, the favorite (because she was favorite for almost everything on the road, track and in cyclo-cross), broke away with three others, and then a fourth joined them later. Each took turns in attacking Vos, to wear her down. Without success. The Dutch woman won the sprint easily, beating another Dutch rider, Ellen van Dijk, and then Emma Johnsson of Sweden and Elisa Longo of Italy.

Vos, talking in her pronounced Brabant accent—she lives an hour's ride from the Belgian border—said after the race: "I think I can give up racing now. I thought I'd never win the Ronde, which everyone in the peloton values as a race, but finally I've done it."

She had been handicapped in earlier races by supporting a teammate or suffering from flu.

"Today it finally worked," she said.

And there is still that rival race, the old *Het Volk*, set up as a protest against the Ronde's alleged collaboration with the Germans.

In theory it should forecast a Ronde winner, held as it is just two weeks beforehand, close enough to show good form, long enough for riders to recover afterward. But it doesn't. The first Het Volk was in 1945.

The first in which there was a link with the Ronde was 1947, when Emiel Faignaert came second in Het Volk and won the Ronde. In 1950 Briek Schotte came third in Het Volk and second in the Ronde. In 1972 André Dierickx came second in both. In 1973 Eddy Merckx won Het Volk and came third in the Ronde. In 1979 Jan Raas came second in Het Volk and then won the Ronde. In 1991 Edwig van Hooydonck came third and then won the Ronde. In 1995 Andrei Tchmil came third in both.

And that's it for the first half a century. Just seven riders. Nobody in 50 years won both. And only two riders who got on the Volk podium then won the Ronde. Of course, that doesn't take into account how many rode both races, nor who saw one race as more important than the other. Riders may have ridden Het Volk as training for the Ronde and without wanting to exhaust themselves. Others may have chosen Het Volk, the less prestigious, because they had the talent to be only team men in the Ronde. Nevertheless, there is no parallel worth considering between the two races.

Het Volk was a tabloid, strong on sport, with editions for all the Flemish provinces and a separate edition for Gent itself. The organizer of Het Volk, the race, was a slim man with dark hair, large oval glasses, a mustache, and a neat beard which covered just his chin. His name was Antoon van Melkebeek. He was the newspaper group's director-general, no less.

Van Melkebeek was in the same position as his rivals at the Ronde. He had a budget—six million francs at the start of the 1990s—and a team which spent a year organizing each race. As soon as one race finished, work started on the next, which made last-minute cancellations because of weather all the more distressing. The two weeks between Het Volk and the Ronde were meteorologically significant, the Ronde getting simply wet and raw weather at worst but Het Volk being canceled several times at the last moment because snow had fallen overnight.

Van Melkebeek tried to change the route every year. That meant a lot of letter-writing because there were 200 mayors to deal with each year. "Some of the mayors are more difficult than others," he said, "but, of course, they all agree in the end. They can refuse because that particular bit of road isn't safe for some reason, and the police agree, but actually refusing, no, they can't do that."

Why?

Because neither Het Volk and its successor nor the Ronde asks for the roads to be closed.

"They can't refuse. It's a public road, isn't it? They can't stop you traveling on a public road. Fully closed roads are unknown in Belgium now. The traffic, the social structure, people's attitudes—they all make closing the road out of the question. So we can't do it. It's already getting more and more difficult to organize big races here and there's pressure to use less busy roads," he said.

"For instance, we have had to move the finish. We used to have it in the center of Gent, but it used to tie up the roads all day. It had started affecting work in the harbor."

The concept that a bike race is just another heavy load moving slowly down the road, that it asks no more nor less priority than a giant transformer on the back of a truck, is hard to grasp in English-speaking countries. Yet the idea that it might be otherwise was a surprise to van Melkebeek.

Not that that has stopped official interference. Drugs have affected the Ronde, disqualifying riders and either elevating others or leaving, as with Lance Armstrong in the Tour de France, just an "X" beside the year. And they affected Het Volk. The British writer, William Fotheringham, wrote of a drugs swoop during the race. The background is that Belgium was the first country to pass what most still don't have: a national law against drugs in sport. It was introduced on April 2 in 1965 and it was applied in a way that suggested an assault against the Mafia.

"All roads into the city [of Gent] were sealed by police," Fotheringham wrote, "all cars involved with the race were searched. The first five finishers were tested, apart from two who 'did not understand the situation.' It was a farce: a vast show of strength which had been easily subverted."

There were more raids, signaled by noise from the police and warning shouts from everyone else. Belgian law forbade only the possession of drugs. That presumed that they were found inside a rider's body by urine tests or in his pockets or luggage by searches. One former independent, or semi-professional, remembered: "You'd be laughing about what you were taking, and feeling each other's pockets to laugh at the syringe you could feel there, and suddenly shouts would go up and you'd know the police had arrived. Then it would suddenly go quiet because people didn't have time to talk, and in a moment all you could hear was the sound of pills bouncing across the floor, and syringes making that dull thump noise as they fell, because we were all emptying our pockets and cases. It cost a fortune, because there was a real market in this stuff, and you'd spend a lot of your earnings on it, but you didn't dare be caught with any.

"The guys nearest the door were most at risk, and nobody wanted to get changed there, but we soon learned to have supporters outside to shout when they saw the cars arrive. The police would muscle round the room and treat us like animals, but there was always a funny side, because if the pills didn't crunch under their boots, they'd go skidding on them and swear worse than we did."

Rik van Steenbergen used to say that the modern Ronde is more demanding and more nervous than in his time. "When I was racing," he said, "the race could be forecast far more easily. In the first half of the race there was usually a windy stretch along the coast that sorted the corn from the chaff. The best riders fought it out man to man in the hills. Now it's much more complex. Now as a rider you have to fight everywhere."

Peter van Petegem says: "The days when Eddy Merckx would attack and ride on his own for 100 kilometers are gone. Winning a classic now is all about waiting and picking your moment."

And, yes, he's right. The days of Merckx have gone. Barry Hoban, a British rider in a break with Merckx in 1969, recalled: "Merckx didn't really attack. He just rode away from us when he went to the front for his spell of pace-making." And that not on a hill but a long straight stretch.

Merckx has changed and so has much else of the Ronde. The grumpy men in flat caps who sit in Belgian bars and divide their interests between cycling and pigeon racing deplore the changes. They suffer from old men's disease. Because to paraphrase the singer, Boxcar Willie, the Ronde never was the race it was. From 1920 to 1938, it rode out to the coast and then turned, with the bleak North Sea to the riders' right. The wind swept in from the water, cold and unhindered, as van Steenbergen described, and the unfortunate riders formed shoulder-to-shoulder lines across the road for protection. These lines, known in Dutch as *waaiers* or fans, are distinctively Flandrian. They were the image of the race. The best got in the front lines and did their best to keep out anyone else.

The *waaier*, or *bordure* in French (the English word, echelon, is unknown in European cycling), has two parallel lines of riders stretched from one edge of the road to the other. The lines are angled into the wind, so that the rider on the front end of the line protects those beside him. After a spell exposed to the wind, the end rider drops back, everyone else moves one space to the side and a fresh rider comes up from the second row to replace him. The tied wind-breaker takes up his place in the second line and waits for his turn to come again.

The easiest way to understand a manoeuvre too complicated to explain in words is to imagine a row of knots on a loop of string. Stretch the loop as wide as it will go, then rotate it around your fingers. Each knot represents a rider. Those in the front will move one way and, one by one, those in the back will replace them. At the other end, a rider will drop into the second line to make more room in front. In that way, each rider braves the wind only at the front of the line.

Sometimes there could be several pairs of lines, the best riders in front and the rest in second and even third formations behind them. Second-hopers who made the front line to the dismay of better riders were engineered, sometimes roughly, out of the group and left to drift back to the chasers. Conversely, to get from one *waaier* to the one in front meant chasing hard, exposed to the wind, using huge energy perhaps only to find the others shouldering him back to his agony.

"The wind was king," Rik Vanwalleghem said of those days. "It would break up the peloton. There was no talk of team tactics in those days: the team system didn't yet exist and riders rode the whole day at full tilt. It was everyone for himself and God against everyone." Not least because for many years the coast road was cobbled.

The tradition of skirting the sea ended when the Germans, who otherwise did their best to keep the race alive, refused access to the coast. The North Sea returned from 1961 to 1963 but then the UCI limited the distance of races after the death of Tom Simpson in the

Tour de France of 1967. That had brought claims that riders took drugs because races were inhumanly long. And moving the start to St-Niklaas meant a trip to the coast would exceed that limit.

Then the sea came back, profiting from moving the start east to Brugge. The organizers wanted to return to their roots, said Vanwalleghem, adding: "It would be really naive to believe that in so doing they'd return to the chaos of the past along the coast. Modern cycling, with its strong teams supported by sponsors, didn't lend itself to such things."

And the course is easier elsewhere, too. Nearly all the first half of the race's history was on cobbles or on roads little better than cobbles. Belgium's post-war determination to asphalt its back roads robbed the race of one obstacle after another. And the Ronde grew less demanding because of that. It may have become faster but the shoulder-barging, thigh-wringing nature of the race had gone, or had at any rate been diluted. There is no such thing as an undeserving winner of the Ronde van Vlaanderen but the 1970s brought not just Merckx and De Vlaeminck but the less memorable Eef Dolman (1971), a good criterium rider and impressive in his day but not a name to change history; Cees Bal (1974), who was no more than a loyal team rider who spotted his chance where others missed theirs; and even Eric Leman in 1970, 1972 and 1973, known until then as a sprinter even if he did win the Ronde alone.

It was because the cobbled climbs were becoming fewer and fewer that the organizers moved to them to the end, to make the most of what they had and the decisions they could force. But the distance of cobbles has fallen for four decades. It was down to 34.5 kilometers in 1977; by 1998 there were only 13.7 kilometers. The climbs have increased but not the cobbles.

Nevertheless, the status of the Ronde is assured. It is so close to the Flemish heart, historically a symbol of Flanders' rise from the "dead land" of Gilles Comte's assessment. Now, for those who read still more into it, it represents the north's final triumph over the south, because now Flanders is rich and Wallonia poor. But it has had a uniting effect as well. Liège–Bastogne–Liège may be older but, even in the French-speaking south, the Ronde is seen as the more colorful, the more spectacular. That unifying effect was recognized in 2013 when the Royal

Mint produced a boxed 10-euro coin with the king's head on one face and a cyclist riding towards a map of Belgium on the other.

The modern Ronde costs €1.5 million to organize. That money is spent on the fee paid to the world cycling body, on prizes (including €20,000 for the winner), expenses for riders who take part, salaries for the full and part-time staff, and a hundred different costs right down to a token fee for the 825 enthusiasts willing to stand at junctions to close side roads to approaching traffic. The money comes from TV rights in Belgium and around the world, commercial sponsors, donations from the government of Flanders and the administration in West Flanders, fees from the cities in which the race starts and ends, and from elsewhere. Merchandising, too, plays a part. Truly determined fans have over the years been able to buy Ronde clothing and even watches.

Organizing the race takes five full-time employees and 2,000 more on the day. There are seven kilometers of advertising banners, 350 advertising placards, two kilometers of fencing and 450 journalists, picked from the 1,500 who ask to be accredited. The publicity caravan ahead of the race stretches from 4 to 15 kilometers according to the stage of the race. It can take 22 minutes to pass.

But one figure tells all about what the Ronde means to Belgians. Sixteen thousand Belgians, each of them unknown, are out testing themselves on the course on the day before the race. They have signed up for the so-called "cycle-tourist" version of the race. There is, for English speakers, some difference between what *they* understand by "cycle-tourist" and what the Flemish are thinking of when they say *wielertouristen*. A glance at the warriors who mass in the market at Brugge at seven on the morning before the Ronde dispels any notion of Pickwickian characters in tweed shorts and checkered shirts. These are men going into battle.

The reputation of the Ronde means that of the 16,000 grim-faced amateurs in Brugge and at Oudenaarde, where the shorter course starts, 6,500 come from abroad, from all five continents. Their importance to Flanders isn't ignored: in 2013 they were greeted at the start by the Flanders president and the federal deputy premier. And by the mayor of Brugge and, says the publicity material, "by the singer, Frederik Sioen."

The unknowns will never ride the Ronde, nor ride as far or as fast as their heroes. But they rattle and struggle just as much and, when they fall, they bleed no less. In their heads, they are stars.

And nobody can steal their dreams.

Start and Finish of the Ronde

Start:

1913–1976	Gent: Mariakerke
1977–1997	St-Niklaas: 't Zand en Markt
1998–	Brugge: St-Kruis

Finish:

1913	Mariakerke track, Gent
1914	Evergem track
1915	Race held on Evergem track
1916–1918	No Ronde
1919–1923	Gentbrugge (Gent), Arsenaal track
1924–1927	Gent, indoor track
1928–1941	Jan Broeckaertlaan, Wetteren
1942–1944	Het Kuipke indoor track, Gent
1945–1951	Jan Broeckaertlaan, Wetteren
1952–1957	Warandelaan, Wetteren
1958–1961	Grote Markt, Wetteren
1962–1963	Emiel Verhaerenlaan, Gentbrugge (Gent)
1964–1972	Merelbeke station, Gent
1973–2010	Halsesteenweg, Meerbeke
2011–	Oudenaarde

Principal Climbs

Where the Ronde climbs; they don't feature in all races:

Climb	Location	Surface	Length (m)	Height gain (m)	Average gradient (%)	Maximum gradient (%)
Berendries	Berendries, St-Maria-Ouden-hove, Brakel	Surfaced	900	65	7.2	14
Berg ten Houte	Tenhoutestraat, Louise-Ma-rie, Maarkedal	Surfaced	1,100	69	6.3	18
Bosberg	Kapellestraat, Geraardsber-gen-Moerbeke	Concrete and then cobbles	475	40	8.4	11
Edalareberg[1]	Vandefonteynelaan, Edalareberg	Surfaced since 1970	1,425	66	4.6	13
Eikenberg	Eikenberg	Cobbles with patches of asphalt	1,175	65	5.5	11
Grotenberge	Grotenbergestraat, Grotenberge	Once cobbled but now surfaced in asphalt and concrete	875	33	3.8	7
Hoogberg	Hoogberg, Zulzeke	Concrete and tar, in two sections with a flat section between them	2,975	105	3.5	8

Les Woodland

Climb	Location	Surface	Length (m)	Height gain (m)	Average gradient (%)	Maximum gradient (%)
Kasteelstraat	Kasteeldreef, St-Maria-Oudenhove, Brakel	Surfaced since 1963	800	52	6.5	8
Kattenberg	Katteberg, Ename, Oudenaarde	Mixed asphalt and cobbles	600	40	6.7	8
Keiweg	Keiweg, Zegelsem	Asphalt with a stretch of cobbles	975	49	5	14
Kloosterstraat	Denderstraat, Abdijstraat, Oude Steenweg, Geraardsbergen	Surfaced	825	77	9.3	17
Kluisberg	Rue des Résistants, Enclus du Haut, starting from Orroir	Asphalt and concrete	1,025	63	6.1	12
Kluisberg	Buissestraat, Bergstraat, Ruien, Kluisbergen, starting from Ruien	Surfaced since 1970s	1,100	66	6	11
Knokteberg[2]	Knoktstraat, Kluisbergen	Surfaced	1,100	88	8	13
Koppenberg[3]	Steengat, Koppenberg	Surfaced and then cobbled	550	64	11.6	25
Kortekeer	Kortekeer, Zulzeke-Nukerke, Maarkedal	Surfaced	1,000	66	6.6	15
Kouterberg	Nameless road in Maarke-Kerkem region	Concrete	1,175	53	4.5	7
Kruisberg	Kruisstraat, Ronse	Surfaced	1,875	90	4.8	9

Climb	Location	Surface	Length (m)	Height gain (m)	Average gradient (%)	Maximum gradient (%)
Kwaremont	Stationsstraat, Ronsebaan, Berchem-Kwaremont	Surfaced	2,550	106	4.2	8
Leberg	Zegelsem	Surfaced	850	39	4.6	15
Molenberg	Molenberg, St-Denijs-Boekel	Cobbles	325	32	9.8	17
Muur	Abdijstraat, Oudebergstraat, Oudeberg, Geraardsbergen (Grammont)	Surfaced, then cobbles	750	68	9.1	20
Muur-Kapelmuur	Abdijstraat, Oudebergstraat, Oudeberg, Geraardsbergen (Grammont)	Surfaced, then cobbles	825	77	9.3	20
Oude Kwaremont	Broektestraat, Kwaremontplein, Schilderstraat, Berchem-Kwaremont	Surfaced, then cobbles	93	93	4.2	11
Paterberg	Paterbergstraat, Kwaremont	Cobbles	375	375	12.8	20
Statieberg	Savooistraat, Nitterveldstraat, Maarkedaal	Surfaced	1,400	52	3.7	9
Steenberg	Steenberg, St-Kornelis-Horebeke	Surfaced since 1981	825	60	7.3	17
Taaienberg	Taaienberg, Etikhove	Cobbles	475	45	9.5	18
Tiegemberg	Vossenhol, Tiegem	Surfaced	750	42	5.6	9
Valkenberg	Valkenbergstraat, Brakel	Surfaced since 1973	875	53	6.1	15

Les Woodland

Climb	Location	Surface	Length (m)	Height gain (m)	Average gradient (%)	Maximum gradient (%)
Varentberg	Varentstraat, Varent	Surfaced, with cobbles at top	1,225	69	5.6	16
Volkegemberg	Volkegemberg, Oudenaarde	Surfaced, with cobbles at top	1,075	54	5	12

1. There is another way to take the hill, without using Vandenfonteylaan. This other approach was used for three years from 1970, the year it was asphalted. It is 100m longer but the maximum is 7%.

2. The same hill can also be climbed from the Ruien direction. It too is surfaced but it starts higher and therefore climbs less—66 meters—for the same distance. Average 6%, maximum 11%.

3. The race traditionally takes the hill from the village side. Approached from the main road, it is surfaced and not difficult.

Index

9 780985 963620